Contents

"Phooey on These Juniors!"
By Abigail Van Buren

Dear Abby: Please print my letter so other mothers won't make the same mistake I did. After 19 years, I realize the error of naming our son after his father.

When he was a baby, it was no problem. We called him Billy and his father was Bill.

When he got older he decided Billy was too baby-ish, so he asked us to call him Bill, which wasn't too bad—we called one Big Bill and the other Little Bill. That worked out fine until Little Bill got bigger than Big Bill.

Now it's worse. It's Young Bill and Old Bill and you can imagine how thrilled father is to be Old Bill at 44.

Not only that, but their voices are identical, and they are constantly being mistaken for one another on the telephone. And their mail gets mixed up, too.

It's a pain in the neck. I should have named him Lawrence, like I wanted to. I've always loved that name. Phooey on these "Juniors."

Too Late Now

Dear Abby

Dear Too: Thanks. New mothers take note.

15 Things to Consider When You Name Your Baby

1. **Namesakes:** Exact reproductions of a parent's name, even if followed by a Jr. or II, can be confusing to everyone involved. Parents may vary the middle name of a son who carries his father's first name and call the son by his middle name, but the potential for confusion still exists. What's worse, the child never gets the satisfaction of having a name and therefore an identity of his very own.

   Namesakes can lead to unhappy choices of names for the child, too. Somehow Mildred doesn't seem appropriate for a little girl, even though it suits 80-year-old Aunt Mildred perfectly. Generally, it is wiser to be certain a namesake's name is one you'd choose on its own merits, quite apart from the good feelings you have for the person you're complimenting this way.

2. **Nationality:** If you choose a foreign-sounding name, be sure it's not a burden to your child by being unpronounceable or unspellable. Multicultural combinations of names, like Françoise Finklebaum, Colleen Kowalski, or Mario Murphy, may provoke smiles. So try out names with different ethnic roots on lots of people before making your final choice (see popular names from around the world, pages 11-13).

3. **Religion:** Some parents think it is important to follow religious traditions in naming a baby. Roman Catholics traditionally choose saints' names, sometimes using Mary as a first name for each daughter and pairing it with different middle names, like Mary Catherine and Mary Margaret. By tradition, Jews prefer biblical names, often the name of a deceased relative; Protestants prefer Old and New Testament names; and Black Muslims prefer Islamic names.

4. **Gender:** Some parents feel that a unisex name, like Robin, Chris, Pat, Carol/Caroll, or Leslie/Lesley, allows them to pick a name with certainty before the baby's sex is known, and that such names are less likely to "type" children in sex roles than traditional gender-specific names. Others argue that it's a nuisance to require a child to explain which sex he or she is. And, gender confusion can cause psychological damage, though studies indicate that boys tend to feel more threatened when they are presumed to be girls than vice versa (remember the song, "A Boy Named Sue"?).

5. Number of Names: Most bureaucratic forms provide spaces for a first name, a middle name, and a last name—but there's no law that requires a person to have three names. There are lots of options: a first and last name only, a first and last name and a middle initial (Harry S Truman's S is just an S), initials for both first and middle names, or several middle names. But if you're thinking of more than three names, consider the problem your child will face every time he or she fills out a form.

6. Sounds: Some names seem to sound better in combination with a last name than others. For example, Julius Caesar sounds better than Jules Caesar and is easier to say. Alliteration, as in Tina Turner or Pat Paulsen, is fine, but rhymes like Jack Black or Wanda Fonda invite teasing. Punning names and other displays of wit may sound funny, but living with a joke name is no laughing matter.

7. Rhythms: Most naming specialists agree that names with unequal num-bers of syllables, like Dwight David Eisenhower, create pleasing rhythms. When first and last names have equal numbers of syllables, a middle name with a different number creates a nice effect, as in Lyndon Baines Johnson. Single-syllable names can be especially forceful if each name has a rather long sound, as in Mark Twain.

8. Pronunciation: Having your name constantly mispronounced would test the patience of a saint. If you pick a foreign name like Jésus or Genviève, don't expect people to pronounce them as they do in the old country (hay-soos and zhan-vee-ev). Other names with high mispronunciation potential are names that have more than one common pronunciation, like Alicia (does the second syllable rhyme with fish or leash?) or Shana (does the name rhyme with Anna or Dana?). And if you choose a unique pronunciation for a name (for example pronouncing Nina like Dinah), don't expect many people to get it right.

9. Spelling: Ordinary spellings have the force of common sense behind them—it is an unneccessary irritation to have your name misspelled. On the other hand, a new and different spelling can give an old name a new twist. Consider how changing the last letter or two affects your impression of Cathy, Cathi, and Cathee. Many people think it's silly to vary from the traditional spelling of names and are prejudiced against any Thom, Dik, or Hari.

10. Popularity: More than 87% of all baby boys and 80% of all baby girls were given one of the 100 most popular names during 1990 (see the most popular boys' and girls' names, pages 7-10). Some names are so popular you shouldn't be surprised to find more than one child with that name in your child's classroom. A child with a very popular name may feel that he or she must "share" it with others, while a child with a very uncommon name is likely to feel that it is uniquely his or hers. However, a child with a popular name is likely to have an easier time gaining acceptance from peers than a child with a very uncommon name, which may be perceived as weird.

11. **Uniqueness:** Did you ever try to look in the phone book for the telephone number of someone named John Smith? You can't find it without knowing the address. To avoid confusion, many people with common last names choose distinctive first and/or middle names for their children. However, a name that is highly unusual, like Teague or Hestia, could be an even greater disservice to your child than James and Jessica.

12. **Stereotypes:** Most names call to mind physical or personality traits that often stem from a well-known namesake, real or fictional. People think of Abe as honest, Albert as fat, Adolph as cruel, Elmer as dumb, Raquel as beautiful, Roseanne as loud, and Erma as funny. Because the image of a name will affect its owner's self-image as well as the way he or she is perceived by others, consider what associations come to mind as you make your selections (see stereotypes of names, pages 4-5).

13. **Nicknames:** Most names have short-ened or familiar forms that are used during childhood or at different stages of life. For example, Michael might be called Mikey as a child, Mike as a teenager, and Michael on his college application. So, if you don't want your daughter called Sam, don't name her Samantha.

If you're leaning in the direction of giving your child a nickname as his or her legal name, remember that Trisha may grow weary of explaining that her real name is not Patricia. And consider the fact that names that sound cute for a child, like Missy and Timmy, could prove embarrassing later on in life. Can you picture Grandma Missy and Grandpa Timmy?

14. **Meanings:** Most names have literal meanings. For example, Jennifer means white or fair; Calvin means bald. If you and your spouse have full heads of red hair, those might be two names to cross off your list. If you have to choose between two names that are equally appealing to you, the meanings may help tip the balance.

15. **Initials:** Before you settle on a first and middle name, consider what your child's initials will be. It can be irksome, even embarrassing, to have DUD or HAG stamped on your suitcases or sweaters. So check out the initials of the names you are thinking of to make sure there's no problem.

Stereotypes of Names

Consciously or unconsciously, we all have private pictures of the people who answer to certain names. Jackie could be sophisticated and beautiful, like Jackie Kennedy or fat and funny like, Jackie Gleason. These pictures come from personal experience as well as from the images we absorb from the mass media and thus may conflict in interesting ways. Charlton strikes many people as a sissified, passive, whiny brat until they think of Charlton Heston. Marilyn may be the personification of voluptuous femininity until you think of your neighbor who fetches the mail in a ratty bathrobe, with curlers in her hair and a cigarette dangling out of her mouth.

Over the years researchers have been fascinated by the "real" meanings of names and their effects on their bearers. Studies indicate that people actually tend to agree on each name's characteristics.

If people think of Mallory as cute and likeable, does that influence a girl named Mallory to become cute and likeable? Experts agree that names don't guarantee instant success or condemn people to certain failure, but they *do* affect self-images, influence relationships with others, and help (or hinder) success in work and school.

Robert Rosenthal's classic experiment identified what he named the Pygmalion effect: randomly selected children who'd been labeled "intellectual bloomers" actually *did* bloom!

Another researcher, S. Gray Garwood, conducted a study of sixth graders in New Orleans. He found that students given names that were popular with teachers scored higher in skills tests, were better adjusted and more consistent in their self-perceptions, were more realistic in their evaluations of themselves, and more frequently expected to attain their goals—even though their goals were more ambitious than ones set by their peers.

In San Diego, research suggested that average essays by Davids, Michaels, Karens, and Lisas got better grades than average essays written by Elmers, Huberts, Adelles, and Berthas. The reason? Teachers expected kids with popular names to do better (the Pygmalion effect again), and thus they assigned higher grades to those kids in a self-fulfilling prophecy.

The largest name study was conducted by the Sinrod Marketing Group's International Opinion panel. They surveyed 75,000 parents to discover their opinions about names. Results of this poll are presented in *The Baby Name Personality Survey* by Bruce Lansky and Barry Sinrod.

Their book contains the names people most often associate with hundreds of adjectives describing personal attributes, such as intelligent, athletic, attractive, and nice (as well as dumb, clutzy, ugly, and nasty). It also contains personality profiles of 1,400 common and unusual boys' and girls' names, and includes real or fictional famous namesakes who may have influenced people's perceptions of each name.

What the authors found was that most names have very clear images; some even have multiple images. Below are some positive attributes and some boys' and girls' names often associated with them.

Attractive

Boys:	Girls:
Adam	Brooke
Blake	Danielle
Christopher	Kimberly
Clint	Nicole
Douglas	Sarah

Intelligent

Boys:	Girls:
Alexander	Agatha
David	Barbara
Edward	Diana
Nelson	Marcella
Samuel	Vanessa

Athletic

Boys:	Girls:
Brian	Chris
Daniel	Katie
Derek	Lindsay
Jake	Jessie
Kevin	Martina

Nice

Boys:	Girls:
Brendan	Donna
Craig	Jill
Joel	Judy
Kenny	Kendra
Todd	Sandy

Many names have negative connotations. Here is a brief list:

Boys	Girls
Adolph (cruel)	Agnes (harsh)
Butch (mean)	Alexis (nasty)
Chuck (bully)	Bertha (fat)
Damian (evil)	Blair (conceited)
Ebenezer (miserly)	Candy (dumb)
Elmer (dumb)	Chloris (cold)
Gustave (arrogant)	Hedda (ugly)
Vernon (weird)	Lola (sleazy)
Vito (gangster)	Velma (mean)

The name you select for your baby is likely to be that child's "label" for a lifetime. It is important to consider how that name will be perceived by others before making your final choice.

The Most Popular Names

The popularity of names, like the length of hemlines and the width of ties, is subject to change every year. The changes become even more noticeable when you think about the changes in name "fashions" over longer periods.

Think about the names of your grandparents and famous entertainers of their generation: Bette Davis, Dorothy Lamour, Rhonda Fleming, Helen Hayes, Margaret O'Brien; Ralph Bellamy, Fred Astaire, Gary Cooper, Frank Sinatra—none of their first names is in the list of top 100 names for 1990.

Popular entertainers of the 1950's included Debbie Reynolds, Troy Donahue, Doris Day, Rock Hudson, and Patti Page—none of their first names is in the list of top 100 names for 1990, either.

It seems that in every decade a new group of names rises in popularity, as names associated with a previous generation of babies decline. So, it is wise to consider whether a name's popularity is on the rise, declining, or holding steady.

To help you assess name popularity trends, we are presenting the top 100 names given to baby boys and girls during 1990, in comparison to their rank during 1989. The rankings are derived from a survey of 8,000 mothers conducted during 1990 by the International Opinion Panel, a division of the Sinrod Marketing Group of Hicksville, New York.

Because you may be wondering how many Michaels and Jessicas you can expect in your child's kindergarten class, we're showing the percentage of all baby boys and girls who are given each name. It may interest you to know that in 1990, 3.5 out of every 100 baby boys were named Michael and 2.8 out of every 100 baby girls were named Jessica.

By checking the percentage of all baby boys or girls who are given each name, you can also gauge the relative popularity of alternate spellings of popular names. For example, Eric is preferred to Erik by more than 4 to 1; Sarah is preferred to Sara by more than 3 to 1.

As you refer to the following data, remember that the popularity issue cuts two ways: 1) Psychologists say a child with a common or popular name seems to have better odds of success in life than a child with an uncommon name. 2) A child whose name is at the top of the popularity poll may not feel as unique and special as a child whose name is less common.

The 100 Most Popular Girls' Names in 1990

1990 Rank	Name	% of girls	1989 Rank	1990 Rank	Name	% of girls	1989 Rank
1.	Jessica	2.8%	6	22.	Danielle	1.1%	20
2.	Sarah	2.2%		23.	Kayla	1.1%	37
	Sara	0.6%		24.	Christina	0.7%	
		2.8%	1		Kristina	0.4%	
3.	Brittany	1.8%				1.1%	28
	Brittney	0.6%		25.	Lynn	1.0%	
	Brittanie	0.1%			Lynne	0.1%	
		2.5%	3			1.1%	12
4.	Ashley	2.5%	5	26.	Victoria	1.1%	39
5.	Amanda	2.3%	—	27.	Jamie	0.7%	
6.	Megan	1.8%			Jaime	0.4%	
	Meghan	0.2%				1.1%	35
		2.0%	9	28.	Rebecca	1.0%	32
7.	Elizabeth	1.8%	17	29.	Erica	1.0%	27
8.	Michelle	0.8%		30.	Lindsey	0.6%	
	Michele	0.8%			Lindsay	0.4%	
		1.6%	15			1.0%	46
9.	Ann	1.0%		31.	Chelsea	0.9%	49
	Anne	0.6%		32.	Emily	0.9%	14
		1.6%	10	33.	Amy	0.9%	40
10.	Samantha	1.5%	36	34.	Katherine	0.7%	
11.	Lauren	1.5%	8		Catherine	0.2%	
12.	Jennifer	1.4%	7			0.9%	2
13.	Renee	1.4%	13	35.	Allison	0.9%	
14.	Kelly	1.1%		36.	Kimberly	0.8%	59
	Kellie	0.2%		37.	Melissa	0.8%	38
	Kelley	0.1%		38.	Brooke	0.4%	
		1.4%	11		Brook	0.4%	
15.	Kristen	0.9%				0.8%	24
	Kristin	0.5%		39.	Heather	0.8%	25
		1.4%	18	40.	Courtney	0.7%	58
16.	Nicole	1.3%	4	41.	Katie	0.7%	—
17.	Alexandra	1.3%	23	42.	Whitney	0.7%	56
18.	Marie	1.3%	16	43.	Marisa	0.7%	55
19.	Cassandra	1.0%		44.	Kelsey	0.7%	42
	Kassandra	0.2%		45.	Tiffany	0.7%	47
		1.2%	33	46.	Caitlin	0.3%	
20.	Rachel	1.2%	22		Katelyn	0.3%	
21.	Stephanie	1.2%	19			0.6%	52

The 100 Most Popular Girls' Names in 1990 (cont.)

1990 Rank	Name	% of girls	1989 Rank	1990 Rank	Name	% of girls	1989 Rank
47.	Mary	0.6%	—	74.	Valerie	0.4%	86
48.	Paige	0.6%	21	75.	Abigail	0.4%	50
49.	Christie	0.4%		76.	Anna	0.4%	48
	Kristi	0.2%		77.	Dawn	0.4%	45
		0.6%	—	78.	Jenny	0.2%	
50.	Amber	0.6%	29		Jenni	0.2%	
51.	Grace	0.6%	54			0.4%	—
52.	Jaclyn	0.3%		79.	Olivia	0.4%	—
	Jacquelyn	0.2%		80.	Pat	0.4%	—
	Jacqueline	0.1%		81.	Dana	0.3%	62
		0.6%	65	82.	Kendra	0.3%	—
53.	Laura	0.6%	31	83.	Kim	0.3%	—
54.	Alyssa	0.6%	—	84.	Margaret	0.3%	77
55.	Cassie	0.6%	—	85.	Patricia	0.3%	—
56.	Lucy	0.5%	—	86.	Alexandria	0.3%	—
57.	Marissa	0.3%		87.	Carla	0.3%	—
	Morissa	0.2%		88.	Christine	0.3%	57
		0.5%	55	89.	Gracie	0.3%	91
58.	Noelle	0.3%		90.	Holly	0.3%	60
	Noel	0.2%		91.	Janet	0.3%	—
		0.5%	—	92.	Natasha	0.3%	—
59.	Natalie	0.5%	—	93.	Alicia	0.2%	
60.	Erin	0.5%	67		Alysha	0.1%	
61.	Alexis	0.5%	66			0.3%	38
62.	Andra	0.5%	40	94.	Casey	0.2%	
63.	Leigh	0.5%	26		Kasey	0.1%	
64.	Lisa	0.5%	68			0.3%	80
65.	Chloe	0.4%	—	95.	Krista	0.2%	
66.	Gabriella	0.4%	70		Christa	0.1%	
67.	Julie	0.4%	41			0.3%	—
68.	Morgan	0.4%	44	96.	Caroline	0.3%	75
69.	Nancy	0.4%	—	97.	Desiree	0.3%	76
70.	Jordan	0.4%	43	98.	Hannah	0.3%	30
71.	Kathleen	0.4%	34	99.	Jill	0.3%	83
72.	Linda	0.4%	93	100.	Pamela	0.3%	—
73.	Sophie	0.4%	—				

Note: In 1990. 80% of all baby girls used one of the names listed above.

The 100 Most Popular Boys' Names in 1990

1990 Rank	Name	% of boys	1989 Rank	1990 Rank	Name	% of boys	1989 Rank
1.	Michael	3.6%	1	22.	Thomas	1.3%	26
2.	Matthew	3.5%	2	23.	Jason	1.3%	34
3.	James	2.2%	4	24.	Sean	0.7%	
4.	Zachary	1.8%			Shawn	0.4%	
	Zachery	0.2%			Shaun	0.2%	
	Zackery	0.1%				1.3%	27
	Zacchary	0.1%		25.	Adam	1.2%	22
		2.2%	21	26.	Lucas	1.0%	
5.	Joshua	2.1%	17		Lukas	0.2%	
6.	Ryan	2.1%	6			1.2%	50
7.	Nicholas	1.8%		27.	Brandon	1.2%	37
	Nickolas	0.2%		28.	Mark	1.2%	40
		2.0%	7	29.	Sam	1.2%	41
8.	Nathan	1.9%	23	30.	Cody	1.0%	—
9.	Steven	1.5%		31.	Alex	1.0%	15
	Stephen	0.4%		32.	Joseph	1.0%	16
		1.9%	13	33.	Travis	1.0%	39
10.	David	1.8%	5	34.	John	0.9%	28
11.	Daniel	1.7%	10	35.	Benjamin	0.9%	25
12.	Tyler	1.7%	—	36.	Max	0.9%	—
13.	Jonathan	1.1%		37.	Timothy	0.9%	33
	Jonathon	0.6%		38.	Kevin	0.9%	20
		1.7%	19	39.	Matt	0.9%	—
14.	Eric	1.3%		40.	William	0.9%	36
	Erik	0.3%		41.	Jordan	0.8%	51
		1.6%	14	42.	Jeffrey	0.8%	32
15.	Justin	1.6%	11	43.	Nathaniel	0.8%	—
16.	Andrew	1.6%	8	44.	Allen	0.5%	
17.	Christopher	1.6%	9		Alan	0.2%	
18.	Brian	0.9%				0.7%	29
	Bryan	0.6%		45.	Dustin	0.7%	35
		1.5%	3	46.	Richard	0.7%	43
19.	Kyle	1.5%	24	47.	Samuel	0.7%	—
20.	Robert	1.5%	12				
21	Jacob	1.4%	18				

The 100 Most Popular Boys' Names in 1990 (cont.)

1990 Rank	Name	% of boys	1989 Rank	1990 Rank	Name	% of boys	1989 Rank
48.	Anthony	0.7%	30	72.	Charles	0.4%	44
49.	Alexander	0.7%	—	73.	Isaac	0.4%	95
50.	Gregory	0.6%	49	74.	Marshall	0.4%	96
51.	Cory	0.5%		75.	Raymond	0.4%	100
	Corey	0.1%		76.	Timmy	0.3%	—
		0.6%	31	77.	Douglas	0.3%	87
52.	Patrick	0.6%	38	78.	Ian	0.3%	77
53.	Jeremy	0.6%	47	79.	Leonard	0.3%	—
54.	Aaron	0.6%	46	80.	Neil	0.3%	82
55.	Lee	0.6%	52	81.	Nick	0.3%	—
56.	Brendon	0.4%		82.	Spencer	0.3%	75
	Brendan	0.1%		83.	Brett	0.3%	—
	Brenden	0.1%		84.	Evan	0.3%	56
		0.6%	55	85.	Harvey	0.3%	80
57.	Phillip	0.5%	60	86.	Jesse	0.3%	—
58.	Martin	0.5%	72	87.	Mike	0.3%	—
59.	Austin	0.5%	61	88.	Brad	0.3%	—
60.	Kenneth	0.5%	42	89.	Casey	0.3%	79
61.	Jared	0.4%		90.	Clayton	0.3%	69
	Jarred	0.1%		91.	Derek	0.3%	58
		0.5%	65	92.	George	0.3%	89
62.	Blake	0.4%	68	93.	Lawrence	0.3%	—
63.	Scott	0.4%	45	94.	Mitchell	0.3%	—
64.	Oscar	0.4%	—	95.	Tony	0.3%	—
65.	Bradley	0.4%	54	96.	Norman	0.3%	—
66.	Caleb	0.4%	94	97.	Vincent	0.3%	92
67.	Gerald	0.4%	71	98.	Glenn	0.2%	—
68.	Peter	0.4%	73	99.	Walter	0.2%	—
69.	Paul	0.4%	48	100.	Dennis	0.2%	—
70.	Seth	0.4%	98				
71.	Wesley	0.4%	74				

Note: In 1990, 87% of all baby boys used one of the names listed above.

The Most Popular Names
Around the World

Family roots, foreign travel and names in the news—all these are giving people new ideas for baby names. The following lists show the equivalents of Tom, Dick and Harry (or Ann, Susan and Elizabeth) from around the world. If you want information from a country not listed, check with its embassy or tourist information office. Incidentally, Mohammed (or Muhammad) is the most commonly given name in the world!

Australia

Alison	Andrew
Amanda	Benjamin
Claire	Christopher
Elizabeth	Daniel
Jennifer	David
Kate	James
Lauren	Matthew
Michelle	Michael
Rebecca	Nicholas
Sarah	Timothy

Canada

Ann(e)	Brian
Carol(e)	David
Christine	Derek
Elizabeth	James
Jacqueline	John
Linda	Matthew
Margaret	Michael
Mary, Marie	Pierre
Patricia	Stephen
Susan	William

China

Bik	Cheung
Chun	Chung
Gschu	Fai
Kwan	Hung
Lai	Keung
Lin	Kong
Ling	On
Mei	Tat
Ping	Tung
Yuk	Wing

Egypt

Aziza	Abdu
Efra	Abdulla
Fatima	Ahmed
Halima	Ali
Huda	Mahmud
Indihar	Mohammed
Intisar	Nassir
Nabila	Saied
Nema	Sami
Rakia	Tewfik
Samira	Yahiya

England

Alexandra	Alexander
Anna	Andrew
Catherine	Christopher
Charlotte	David
Elizabeth	James
Emma	Jonathan
Lucy	Nicholas
Rebecca	Robert
Sarah	Thomas
Victoria	William

France

Brigitte	Bernard
Denise	Bruno
Francoise	Didier
Jeanette	Eduard
Laure	Jacques
Marie	Jean
Mariette	Joseph
Michelle	Marc
Nicole	Max
Sophie	Stephan

Germany

Barbara	Claus
Brigitte	Ernst
Claudia	Gunter
Elfie	Johann
Gretchen	Karl
Heidi	Ludwig
Hilda	Peter
Hildegard	Thomas
Mina	Walter
Sandra	Wilhelm

Greece

Angeline	Aristotle
Aphrodite	Christos
Athena	Constantine
Chrisoula	Dimitri
Christina	Kyriako
Emalia	Nicholas
Helena	Panayiotis
Kaliope	Thanasi
Katina	Theodor
Stamata	Yeorgi

Ireland

Brenna	Brendan
Bridget	Colin
Colleen	Curran
Fiona	Darcy
Flanna	Devin
Kathleen	Dillon
Maeve	Liam
Maureen	Owen
Megan	Seamus
Tara	Sean

Israel

Dalia	Benyamin
Daphna	Ehud
Michal	Gal
Orit	Leor
Orly	Oren
Sharon	Roee
Sheeree	Ronen
Tal	Yaakov
Tamar	Yaron
Yael	Yonatan

Italy

Angelina	Antonio
Anna-Maria	Carmelo
Catherina	Eugenio
Costanzia	Francesco
Giovanna	Giuseppe
Lucia	Liborio
Maria	Pasquale
Maria-Giuseppe	Rosario
Rosina	Saberio
Teresa	Salvatore

Japan

Hiroko	Akira
Junko	Hiroshi
Keiko	Kenji
Mariko	Masao
Michiko	Tadashi
Reiko	Takashi
Sachiko	Takeo
Toshiko	Takeshi
Yoko	Yoshio
Yoshiko	Yuji

Mexico

Alicia	Alfonso
Alma	Enrique
Carmen	Fernando
Cristina	Javier
Elena	Jesus
Juana	Juan
Maria	Luis
Marta	Mario
Rosa	Pablo
Susana	Pedro

New Zealand

Anna	Andrew
Emma	Christopher
Jessica	Craig
Kylie	Daniel
Lisa	David
Melissa	Jason
Nicola	Matthew
Rebecca	Michael
Sarah	Nicholas
Stacey	Timothy

Nigeria

Abebi	Adebayo
Akanke	Adigun
Alake	Ajani
Aniweta	Akins
Asabi	Ayo
Fayola	Chinua
Femi	Gowon
Limber	Okechuku
Oba	Orji
Oni	Tor

Norway

Astrid	Anders
Berta	Dag
Dagmar	Erik
Erna	Gunnar
Grete	Hans
Hilde	Ingvar
Inga	Jens
Kari	Karl
Merete	Olaf
Signe	Rolf

Philipines

Aida	Antonio
Alicia	Carlos
Ana	Domingo
Aurora	Francisco
Belen	Jose
Carmen	Juan
Concepcion	Manuel
Leonor	Mariano
Maria	Pedro
Teresa	Ramon

Poland

Aniela	Andrej
Anna	Boleslaw
Eugenia	Eugeniusz
Franciscka	Franek
Jadwiga	Janos
Joana	Karol
Karolina	Lukasz
Lucia	Marian
Marinna	Mateusz
Marta	Tomasz

Portugal

Ana	Antonio
Helena	Fernando
Ines	Filipe
Isabel	Francisco
Luisa	Henrique
Margarida	Joao
Maria	Jose
Rita	Luis
Sofia	Manuel
Teresa	Pedro

Russia

Galina	Alexi
Irina	Dmitri
Larisa	Feodor
Lyudmila	Igor
Marina	Ivan
Natalya	Konstantin
Olga	Nicolai
Sofia	Oleg
Tatiana	Vladimir
Yelena	Yuri

Sweden

Anna	Anders
Britta	Bjorn
Christina	Erik
Elisabeth	Gunnar
Eva	Gustaf
Ingrid	Hans
Karin	Lars
Margareta	Nils
Ulla	Oskar
Ulrika	Per

Baby Name Legal Guide

Shortly after your baby is born someone on the hospital staff will ask you for information to fill out a birth certificate. If your baby is not born in a hospital, either by choice or accident, you still need to file a birth certificate. If you're on your way but don't make it to the hospital in time, the hospital will still take care of filling in the form and presenting it for your signature after you're admitted. If you plan a home birth, you will have to go to the vital statistics office and file a form there—see what your local laws require.

Basic facts about both parents' names, places and dates of birth, and details about the baby like its sex, weight, length, exact time of arrival, and date of birth will be needed for a birth certificate. Questions regarding other children (if any), their ages, previous miscarriages or children's deaths, the educational levels of both parents, and so on might be asked at this time for records at your local division of vital statistics. They may not appear on the actual birth certificate, though.

The hospital staffer will type up the form and present it for the mother and doctor to sign before sending it to the vital statistics division to be recorded permanently. Once it's recorded you can request copies (needed for things like passports, some jobs and some legal transactions).

That's what happens in the usual chain of events. But what about the technicalities and specific legal aspects of naming a child? The first thing to know is that *laws that govern baby naming vary greatly throughout the country*. If your choice of names is in any way unusual (such as giving your baby a hyphenated surname combining the mother's maiden name with the father's name) be sure of the law before you name the baby. And sign the official birth certificate only after it has been filled out to your satisfaction.

A few of the most commonly asked questions concerning legalities are considered here but since state and territory laws are not uniform, even these answers cannot be definite. Your local municipal health department officials can probably lead you to the proper department or official to handle your particular situation. Contact them if you need more detailed answers to your questions.

Q. Are there any restrictions on the choice of first and middle names for a baby?

A. No, with the possible exception that the baby's names should be composed of letters, not numbers. In 1978 a district court judge refused to allow a young Minneapolis social studies teacher to legally change his name to the number 1069, calling such a change "an offense to human dignity" that would "hasten that day in which we all become lost in faceless numbers."

Freedom in choosing given names is not universal. A spokesperson for the French consulate in Chicago confirmed that an 1813 French law still governs naming practices in France. It decrees that babies must be named after Catholic saints or "persons known in ancient history."

Q. Is a choice allowed in giving the baby its surname?

A. In former generations a baby's surname was not often considered a matter for personal decision. If the parents were married, the baby's surname was that of its father. If not, the baby was often assigned the mother's surname.

Today, with many women retaining their maiden names after marriage and others hyphenating their own and their husbands' names, some complications have arisen. As one state health department official said, "The computer does not accept hyphens."

While most states allow parents to select any surname they wish for their babies, current laws in others do not reflect these changes in society. In at least one state—Utah—a special set of guidelines for surname choice has been drawn up.

Some states still require that in the case of married parents, the father's name *must* be used. In some of these states, if the parents are not married the mother's name must be given. In others, the mother may choose her own child's surname.

Q. Must the baby's full name be decided upon before the birth certificate can be registered?

A. Not in most cases. The time limits during which given names must be recorded vary in states and territories from ten days to seven years.

Q. How can a baby's name be legally changed after its birth is registered?

A. More than 50,000 Americans ask courts to change their names legally every year. Some of these changes are requested by parents for their children when the names originally chosen no longer suit them.

Changes in a minor child's given names are possible in some states without a court order, with time limits ranging from a few days after birth to any time at all. In some states a simple affidavit signed by the parents or a notarized amendment is sufficient to make a name change. Others require various documents to show proof of an established new name such as a baptismal certificate, an insurance policy, an immunization record or the family Bible record. For older children, school records or the school census are usually allowed.

When court procedures are necessary they involve petitions to a county probate court, a superior court or a district court, following state laws. Often prior newspaper publication of the intended change is required. The court then issues a "change of name" order or decree. In some states new birth certificates are issued for name changes. In others, certificates are only amended.

Informal name changes can be and often are made simply through the "common law right of choice," which allows individuals to use any names they choose. Such a change *is* informal, though, and is not legal in official procedures.

Q. What if a mistake is made in the baby's name on the birth certificate?

A. To repeat: the best advice of all is to avoid such an occurrence by being absolutely sure that the completely filled-out certificate is correct in every detail before signing it. If a mistake is made, it is important to handle the matter quickly. Procedures for corrections on certificates vary; sometimes signatures of the parents are sufficient but in other cases forms must be filled out or documentary evidence supplied.

Q. What are the laws for renaming adopted children?

A. An adoption decree is a court order legally obtained through basically similar procedures in all states and territories. A child's given names are selected by the adoptive parents and the surname is chosen in accordance with whatever state or territory laws exist for surnames of biological children. Then all these names are recorded in the adoption decree. In most places an entirely new birth certificate is drawn up, although the place of birth is not usually changed. Most often the original birth certificate is sealed with the adoption papers, and the new certificate is filed in place of the original.

Q. How may a child's name be changed by a stepfather, by foster parents, or in the case of legitimization?

A. In the case of a name change related to a stepfather, most states require that individuals follow whichever of the procedures for adoption or for legal change of name is appropriate. There are some exceptions. In Pennsylvania, for example, if a stepfather does not adopt his wife's child, the mother (as "custodial biological parent") may change a child's surname through its seventh year.

The requirements for surname change in the case of a foster child are similar: legal change of name or adoption.

Changing a child's surname in the case of legitimization is virtually the same as the adoption procedure in most states and territories. Some require both an affidavit of paternity *and* a copy of the parents' marriage license, while others do not concern themselves with the marriage of the parents. In California there are no procedures whatsoever, since illegitimacy is no longer defined in that state.

The Name Exchange
★ Celebrities' Names Before and After ★

Professional Name	Original Name	Professional Name	Original Name
Eddie Albert	Edward Albert Heimberger	Robert Blake	Michael James Vijencio Gubitosi
Muhammad Ali	Cassius Marcellus Clay, Jr.	Blondie	Deborah Harry
Woody Allen	Allen Konigsberg	Sonny Bono	Salvatore Bono
Julie Andrews	Julia Vernon	Pat Boone	Charles Eugene Boone
Ann-Margret	Ann-Margret Olsson	David Bowie	David Jones
Beatrice Arthur	Bernice Frankel	Beau Bridges	Lloyd Vernet Bridges III
Fred Astaire	Frederick Austerlitz	Charles Bronson	Charles Buchinsky
Lauren Bacall	Betty Joan Perski	Mel Brooks	Melvin Kaminsky
Lucille Ball	Dianne Belmont	Yul Brynner	Taidje Kahn, Jr.
Anne Bancroft	Anne Italiano	George Burns	Nathan Birnbaum
John Barrymore	John Blythe	Ellen Burstyn	Edna Rae Gillooly
Orson Bean	Dallas Frederick Burrows	Richard Burton	Richard Jenkins
Tony Bennett	Anthony Dominick Benedetto	Michael Caine	Maurice Micklewhite
Jack Benny	Joseph Kubelsky	Maria Callas	Maria Anna Sophia Cecilia Kalogeropoulos
Robby Benson	Robert Segal	Vicki Carr	Florencia Bisenta de Casillas Martinez Cardona
Polly Bergen	Nellie Paulina Burgin		
Ingmar Bergman	Ernst Ingmar Bergman	Diahann Carroll	Carol Diahann Johnson
Milton Berle	Milton Berlinger	Ray Charles	Ray Charles Robinson
Irving Berlin	Israel Baline	Charo	Maria Rosaria Pilar Martinez Molina Baeza
Yogi Berra	Lawrence Peter Berra	Cher	Cherilyn La Pierre
Joey Bishop	Joseph Abraham Gottlieb	Chubby Checker	Ernest Evans
		Eric Clapton	Eric Clap

Professional Name	Original Name	Professional Name	Original Name
Lee J. Cobb	Leo Jacob	**Werner Erhard**	Jack Rosenberg
Perry Como	Pierino Como	**Dale Evans**	Francis Octavia Smith
Bert Convy	Bernard Whalen Patrick Convy	**Chad Everett**	Raymond Lee Cramton
Alice Cooper	Vincent Damon Furnier	**Douglas Fairbanks** .	Julius Ullman
Howard Cosell	Howard William Cohen	**Donna Fargo**	Yvonne Vaughn
Joan Crawford	Lucille Le Sueur	**W.C. Fields**	William Dukenfield
Bing Crosby	Harry Lillis Crosby	**Dame Margot Fonteyn**	Margaret Hookham
Tony Curtis	Bernard Schwartz	**Gerald Ford**	Leslie Lynch King, Jr.*
Rodney Dangerfield	John Cohen	**Glenn Ford**	Gwllyn Samuel Newton Ford
Dawn	Joyce Elaine Vincent	**John Forsythe**	John Freund
Doris Day	Doris Kappelhoff	**Redd Foxx**	John Elroy Sanford
Kiki Dee	Pauline Matthews	**Anthony Franciosa**	Anthony Papaleo
Sandra Dee	Alexandra Zuck	**Connie Francis**	Concetta Franconero
John Denver	Henry John Deutschendorf, Jr.	**Carlton Fredericks** .	Harold Casper Frederick Kaplan
Bo Derek	Mary Cathleen Collins Derek	**Greta Garbo**	Greta Gustafson
Marlene Dietrich ..	Maria von Losch	**Ava Gardner**	Lucy Johnson
Phyllis Diller	Phyllis Driver	**Judy Garland**	Frances Gumm
Kirk Douglas	Issur Danielovitch	**James Garner**	James Baumgarner
Mike Douglas	Michael Delaney Dowd, Jr.	**Crystal Gayle**	Brenda Gail Webb Gatzimos
Patty Duke	Anna Marie Duke	**Ben Gazzara**	Benjamin Antonio Gazzara
Fay Dunaway	Dorothy Faye Dunaway	**Boy George**	George O'Dowd
Bob Dylan	Robert Zimmerman	**Barry Gibb**	Douglas Gibb
Buddy Ebsen	Christian Ebsen, Jr.	**Cary Grant**	Archibald Leach
Samantha Eggar ..	Victoria Louise Eggar	**Lee Grant**	Lyova Haskell Rosenthal
Mama Cass Elliot ..	Ellen Naomi Cohen		

*Gerald Ford took the name of his adoptive parents.

Professional Name	Original Name	Professional Name	Original Name
Peter Graves	Peter Arness	**Ann Landers**	Esther "Eppie" Pauline Friedman Lederer
Joel Gray	Joel Katz		
Buddy Hackett	Leonard Hacker	**Michael Landon**	Michael Orowitz
Halston	Roy Halston Frowick	**Stan Laurel**	Arthur Stanley Jefferson Laurel
Rex Harrison	Reginald Cary		
Gary Hart	Gary Hartpence	**Steve Lawrence**	Sidney Leibowitz
Laurence Harvey ...	Lavrushka Skikne	**John Le Carré**	John Moore Carnwell
Helen Hayes	Helen Brown	**Gypsy Rose Lee** ...	Louise Hovick
Margaux Hemingway	Margot Hemmingway	**Peggy Lee**	Norma Egstrom
Audrey Hepburn ...	Audrey Hepburn-Ruston	**Jerry Lewis**	Joseph Levitch
		Liberace	Wladziu Valentino Liberace
William Holden	William Beedle		
Billie Holiday	Eleanora Fagan	**Hal Linden**	Hal Lipshitz
Bob Hope	Leslie Townes Hope	**Meat Loaf**	Marvin Lee Aday
Harry Houdini	Ehrich Weiss	**Jack Lord**	J.J. Ryan
Rock Hudson	Roy Scherer, Jr.	**Sophia Loren**	Sophia Scicoloni
Engelbert Humperdinck	Arnold Dorsey	**Peter Lorre**	Laszlo Loewenstein
		Myrna Loy	Myrna Williams
Lauren Hutton	Mary Laurence Hutton	**Bela Lugosi**	Arisztid Olt
Kareem Abdul-Jabbar	Ferdinand Lewis Alcindor, Jr.	**Shirley MacLaine** ...	Shirley Beaty
		Paul McCartney	James Paul McCartney
Wolfman Jack	Robert Smith	**Steve McQueen**	Terence Stephen McQueen
Elton John	Reginald Kenneth Dwight	**Madonna**	Madonna Louise Ciccone
Al Jolson	Asa Yoelson		
Tom Jones	Thomas Jones Woodward	**Karl Malden**	Mladen Sekulovich
		Jayne Mansfield	Vera Jane Palmer
Louis Jourdan	Louis Gendre	**Fredric March**	Frederick Bickel
Garson Kanin	Gershon Labe	**Dean Martin**	Dino Crocetti
Boris Karloff	William Pratt	**Chico Marx**	Leonard Marx
Danny Kaye	David Kaminsky	**Groucho Marx**	Julius Henry Marx
Diane Keaton	Diane Hall	**Harpo Marx**	Arthur Marx
Ted Knight	Tadeus Wladyslaw Konopka	**Zeppo Marx**	Herbert Marx
		Walter Matthau	Walter Matuschanskayasky
Bert Lahr	Irving Lahrheim	**Ethel Merman**	Ethel Zimmerman

Professional Name	Original Name	Professional Name	Original Name
Joni Mitchell	Roberta Joan Anderson Mitchell	**Susan Saint James**	Susan Miller
Marilyn Monroe	Norma Jean Baker	**Soupy Sales**	Milton Hines
Yves Montand	Ivo Livi	**Leo Sayer**	Gerald Sayer
Rita Moreno	Rosita Dolores Alverio	**John Saxon**	Carmen Orrico
Zero Mostel	Samuel Joel Mostel	**Tom Seaver**	George Thomas Seaver
Ricky Nelson	Eric Hilliard Nelson	**Omar Sharif**	Michael Shalhouz
Mike Nichols	Michael Igor Peschkowsky	**Artie Shaw**	Arthur Arshowsky
Stevie Nicks	Stephanie Nicks	**Dinah Shore**	Frances "Fanny" Rose Shore
Kim Novak	Marilyn Paul Novak	**Beverly Sills**	Belle "Bubbles" Silverman
Hugh O'Brien	Hugh J. Krampe	**O.J. Simpson**	Orenthal James Simpson
Tony Orlando	Michael Anthony Orlando Cassavitis	**Phoebe Snow**	Phoebe Loeb
Peter O'Toole	Seamus O'Toole	**Suzanne Somers**	Suzanne Mahoney
Satchel Paige	Leroy Robert Paige	**Elke Sommer**	Elke Schletz
Jack Palance	Walter Palanuik	**Sissy Spacek**	Mary Elizabeth Spacek
Gregory Peck	Eldred Gregory Peck	**Mickey Spillane**	Frank Morrison
Pele	Edson Arantes do Nascimento	**Sylvester Stallone**	Michael Sylvester Stallone
Bernadette Peters	Bernadette Lazarra	**Ringo Starr**	Richard Starkey
Paula Prentiss	Paula Ragusa	**Connie Stevens**	Concetta Anne Ingolia
Prince	Roger Nelson	**Sting**	Gordon Summer
William Proxmire	Edward William Proxmire	**Sly Stone**	Sylvester Stone
Ahmad Rashad	Bobby Moore	**Meryl Streep**	Mary Louise Streep
Della Reese	Delloreese Patricia Early	**Donna Summer**	La Donna Andrea Gaines
Lee Remick	Ann Remick	**Mr. T**	Lawrence Tureaud
Debbie Reynolds	Mary Frances Reynolds	**Robert Taylor**	Spangler Brugh
Harold Robbins	Francis Kane	**Danny Thomas**	Amos Jacobs
Edward G. Robinson	Emanuel Goldenberg	**Tiny Tim**	Herbert Buckingham Khaury
Ginger Rogers	Virginia McMath	**J.R.R. Tolkien**	John Ronald Reuel Tolkien
Roy Rogers	Leonard Slye		
Mickey Rooney	Joe Yule, Jr.		
Buffy Sainte-Marie	Beverly Sainte-Marie		

Professional Name	Original Name	Professional Name	Original Name
Lily Tomlin	Mary Jean Tomlin	**Tuesday Weld**	Susan Kerr Weld
Leon Trotsky	Lev Davydovich Bronstein	**Nathaniel West**	Nathaniel Wallenstein Weinstein
Gene Tunney	James Joseph Tunney	**Tennessee Williams**	Thomas Lanier Williams
Twiggy	Leslie Hornby	**Flip Wilson**	Clerow Wilson
Rudolph Valentino	Rudolpho D'Antonguolla	**Woodrow Wilson**	Thomas Woodrow Wilson
Rudy Vallee	Hubert Prior Vallée	**Shelly Winters**	Shirley Schrift
Abigail Van Buren	Pauline Esther "Popo" Friedman Phillips	**Stevie Wonder**	Steveland Morris Hardaway
Gore Vidal	Eugene Vidal	**Natalie Wood**	Natasha Gurdin
Nancy Walker	Ann Myrtle Swoyer	**Jane Wyman**	Sarah Jane Fulks
Mike Wallace	Myron Wallace	**Tammy Wynette**	Wynette Pugh
Andy Warhol	Andrew Warhola	**Ed Wynn**	Isaiah Edwin Leopold
Muddy Waters	McKinley Morganfield	**Cy Young**	Denton True Young
John Wayne	Marion Michael Morrison	**Loretta Young**	Gretchen Young
Raquel Welch	Raquel Tejada		

Fascinating Facts about Names

Birthrights

In some tribal societies children are not considered born until they are named. Frequently the child's name consists of a statement (that is, rather than having a pool of names as Western culture does, parents in these societies name children with a phrase that describes the circumstances of the child's birth, the family's current activities, and so on). Translated, such names might be "We are glad we moved to Memphis," or "A girl at last," or "Too little rain."

Bible Studies

It's been estimated that the majority of people in the Western hemisphere have names based on biblical ones. Women outnumber men, yet there are 3,037 male names in the Bible and only 181 female names. The New Testament is a more popular source of names than is the Old Testament.

Change of Habit

Popes traditionally choose a new name upon their election by the College of Cardinals. The practice began in 844 A.D. when a priest whose real name was Boca de Porco (Pig's Mouth) was elected. He changed his name to Sergious II.

Saint Who?

Saints' names are a common source of names in the U.S. But saints who are popular in other countries contribute very unusual, even unpronounceable, names for children born in the U.S.—like Tamjesdegerd, Borhedbesheba and Jafkeranaegzia.

Them Bones

Praise-God Barebones had a brother named If-Christ-Had-Not-Died-For-Thee-Thou-Wouldst-Have-Been-Damned, who was called "Damned Barebones" for short.

Hello, God?

Terril William Clark is listed in the phone book under his new name—God. Now he's looking for someone to publish a book he's written. "Let's face it," he reportedly said. "The last book with my name on it was a blockbuster."

The Status Quo

The most commonly given names in English-speaking countries from about 1750 to the present are drawn from a list with only 179 entries (discounting variations in spelling). Essentially the same practice has been followed in naming children since at least the 16th century, though the use of middle names has increased over the years.

It's Mainly Relative

A recent study suggests that about two-thirds of the population of the U.S. is named to honor somebody. Of the people who are namesakes, about 60 percent are named after a relative and 40 percent for someone outside the family.

Once Is Enough!

Ann Landers writes of a couple who has six children, all named Eugene Jerome Dupuis, Junior. The children answer to One, Two, Three, Four, Five and Six, respectively. Can you imagine what the IRS, the Social Security Administration, and any other institution will do with the Dupuises?

In Sickness and Health

Tonsilitis Jackson has brothers and sisters named Meningitis, Appendicitis and Peritonitis.

The Old College Try

A couple in Louisiana named their children after colleges: Stanford, Duke, T'Lane, Harvard, Princeton, Auburn and Cornell. The parents' names? Stanford, Sr., and Loyola.

Peace at All Costs

Harry S Truman owed his middle name, the initial S, to a compromise his parents worked out. By using only the initial, they were able to please both his grandfathers, whose names were Shippe and Solomon.

Initials Only

A new recruit in the U.S. Army filled out all the forms he was presented with as he always had in school: R. (only) B. (only) Jones. You guessed it—from then on he was, as far as the Army cared about it, Ronly Bonly Jones, and all his records, dogtags and discharge papers proved the point again and again.

Sticks & Stones May Break My Bones...

The nicknames children make up for each other tend to fall into four patterns: those stemming from the physical appearance of the child, those based on either real or imaginary mental traits (brains or idiocy), those based on social ranking or other relationships, and finally, those based on plays on the child's name. Children who don't conform to the values or looks of their peers are likely to pick up more nicknames than those who conform more uniformly. In these ways nicknames may actually become instruments of social control.

| The Name's the Game | John Hotvet, of Minnetonka, Minnesota, is—of course—a veterinarian. Sometimes names and occupations get inextricably interwoven. Consider these names and professions: |

Dr. Zoltan Ovary, gynecologist
Mr. A. Moron, Commissioner of Education for the Virgin Islands
Reverend Christian Church and Reverend God
Mr. Thomas Crapper of Crapper, Ltd Toilets, in London, who entitled his autobiography *Flushed with Pride*
Assorted physicians named Doctor, Docter or Doktor
Cardinal Sin, Archbishop of Manila, the Philippines
Mr. Firmin A. Gryp, banker of Northern California Savings & Loan Association in Palo Alto, California
Mr. Groaner Digger, undertaker in Houston
Mr. I. C. Shivers, iceman
Ms. Justine Tune, chorister in Westminster Choir College, Princeton New Jersey
Ms. Lavender Sidebottom, masseuse at Elizabeth Arden's in New York City
Mssrs. Lawless and Lynch, attorneys in Jamaica, New York
Major Minor, U.S. Army
Diana Nyad, champion long-distance swimmer
Mssrs. Plummer and Leek, plumbers in Sheringham, Norfolk, England
Mr. Ronald Supena, lawyer
Mrs. Screech, singing teacher in Victoria, British Columbia
Mr. Vroom, motorcycle dealer in Port Elizabeth, South Africa
Mssrs. Wyre and Tapping, detectives in New York City

Time Capsule Names

Celebrities and events often inspire parents in their choices of names for children. Many parents these days are "dated" by their World War II names, like Pearl (Harbor), Douglas (MacArthur), Dwight (Eisenhower—whose mother named him Dwight David to avoid all nicknames, but who wound up with a son everyone called Ike!), and Franklin (Roosevelt). Films and film stars contribute their share of names: Scarlett O'Hara and Rhett Butler have countless namesakes whose parents were swept away by *Gone with the Wind*. Marlon Brando, Farrah Fawcett and virtually every other big star have their own namesakes as well.

They Add Up

Dick Crouser likes to collect names that add up to something. Some names tell stories, like Fanny Pistor Bodganoff (although Mr. Crouser admits that he doesn't know what a "bodgan" is); some leave messages, like Hazel Mae Call; some aren't likely to add to their owner's self-esteem, like Seldom Wright and Harley Worthit; some are mere truisms, like Wood Burns; while other announce what you might call philosophies of life, like Daily Goforth and Hazel B. Good.

Truth Stranger than Fiction

Dick Neff, columnist of *Advertising Age*, invited his readers to contribute lists of real names they had encountered which are odd and/or funny, to say the least. Among them were the following: Stanley Zigafoose, Cigar Stubbs, Ladorise Quick, Mad Laughinhouse, Lester Chester Hester, Effie Bong, Dillon C. Quattlebaum, Twila Szwrk, Harry E. Thweatt, Benjamin E. Dymshits, Elmer Ploof, Whipple Filoon, Sweetie Belle Rufus, Peculiar Smith, John Dunwrong, All Dunn, Willie Wunn, H. Whitney Clappsaddle, W. Wesley Muckenfuss, Rudolph J. Ramstack, Sarabelle Scraper Roach, James R. Stufflebeam, Shanda Lear, Arthur Crudder, Mary Crapsey, Memory Lane, Troy Mumpower, Santa Beans, Sividious Stark, Cleveland Biggerstaff, Trinkle Bott, Cleopatra Barksdale, Spring Belch, Fairy Blessing, Royal Fauntleroy Butler, Bozy Ball, Carl W. Gigl, Joy Holy, Peenie Fase, Che Che Creech, J. B. Outhouse, Katz Meow, Stephanie Snatchole, I. O. Silver, Helen Bunpain, Birdie Fawncella Feltis, Elight Starling, Farmer Slusher, Nebraska Minor, Bill Grumbles, Peter Rabbitt, Carbon Petroleum Dubbs, Kick-a-hole-in-the-soup, Wong Bong Fong, Newton Hooton, Sonia Schmeckpeeper, Lewie Wirmelskirchen, Lolita Beanblossom, Liselotte Pook, and Irmgard Quapp.

Pop-ular Names?

In 1979, the Pennsylvania Health Department discovered these two first names among the 159,000 birth certificates issued in the state that year—Pepsi and Cola.

A Boy Named Sue

Researchers have found that boys who had peculiar first names had a higher incidence of mental problems than boys with common ones; no similar correlation was found for girls.

He Who Quacks Last

In a government check of a computer program, researchers turned up a real-life Donald Duck. It seems that programmers used his name to create a bogus G.I. to check out records—and found out he really existed. The Army Engineer won fame and a visit to the Johnny Carson Show as a result of this discovery.

Too-o-o-o Much!

Many people dislike their own names. The most common reasons given for this dislike are that the names "sound too ugly," that they're old-fashioned, too hard to pronounce, too common, too uncommon, too long, sound too foreign, are too easy for people to joke about, and that they sound too effeminate (for men) or too masculine (for women).

Last But Not Least

Zachary Zzzzra has been listed in the Guinness Book of World Records as making "the most determined attempt to be the last personal name in a local telephone directory" in San Francisco. That happened before his place was challenged by one Vladimir Zzzzzzabakov. Zzzzra reports that he called Zzzzzzabakov and demanded to know his real name (Zzzzra's name is really his own, he says). Zzzzzzabakov told him it was none of his . . . business. At any rate, true to his reputation for determination, Zzzzra changed his name to regain his former — or latter? — position. When the new phone book appeared, he was relieved to find himself comfortably in the last place again, as Zachary Zzzzzzzzzzra. Unknown to him, the contender, Zzzzzzabakov, had disappeared.

The End

One family which was not terribly successful in limiting its expansion has a series of children called, respectively, Finis, Addenda, Appendix, Supplement and (last but not least) Errata.

Birthstones and Flowers

January

Birthstone: **garnet**

Flower: carnation

February

Birthstone: **amethyst**

Flower: violet

March

Birthstone: **aquamarine**

Flower: jonquil

April

Birthstone: **diamond**

Flower: sweet pea

May

Birthstone: **emerald**

Flower: lily of the valley

June

Birthstone: **pearl**

Flower: rose

July

Birthstone: **ruby**

Flower: larkspur

August

Birthstone: **peridot**

Flower: gladiolus

September

Birthstone: **sapphire**

Flower: aster

October

Birthstone: **opal**

Flower: calendula

November

Birthstone: **topaz**

Flower: chrysanthemum

December

Birthstone: **turquoise**

Flower: narcissus

The Baby Name List

This list will provide over 13,000 choices for you to consider as you decide what you'll name your baby. It is intended to be the most useful and contemporary list available. Here are some sample entries that explain how the list works:

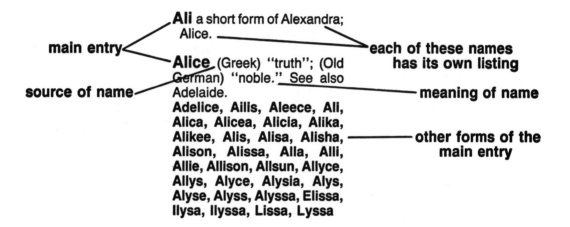

main entry

Ali a short form of Alexandra; Alice.

each of these names has its own listing

source of name

Alice (Greek) "truth"; (Old German) "noble." See also Adelaide.

meaning of name

Adelice, Ailis, Aleece, Ali, Alica, Alicea, Alicia, Alika, Alikee, Alis, Alisa, Alisha, Alison, Alissa, Alla, Alli, Allie, Allison, Allsun, Allyce, Allys, Alyce, Alysia, Alys, Alyse, Alyss, Alyssa, Elissa, Ilysa, Ilyssa, Lissa, Lyssa

other forms of the main entry

One of the most fruitful sources of names for this list was published birth announcements in newspapers from all over the country. The names that turned up in the papers give the list a distinctively contemporary flavor that also reflects regional preferences. In the South, for instance, parents are much more apt to name a baby with what Northerners would call a nickname, like Bessie or Bobbie, while Easterners seem to favor traditional and French variants of traditional names. These birth announcements also showed that parents are creating many new variations and spellings, like Cyndie or Mychal, which are included.

Separate entries appear in this list for many names that older books note only as "nicknames," because names like Jenny, Terry, Beth or Mickey are appearing on birth certificates all over the country! You'll notice that words like "nickname," "pet name," "diminutive," and so on are not used, to avoid suggesting that you shouldn't use a certain name because it isn't a traditional given name. Instead, you'll find more informative phrases like "a Russian short form," "a familiar form," "a feminine form," and so on.

Some of the feminine forms of traditionally male names are identified for you, since you may not recognize the connections—Charlotte *is* a form of Charles that most people overlook.

Surnames are becoming popular as first names these days. You'll see many in this list, especially ones that have come to be "standard" first names, like Logan, Carter, Parker and Reed. But if you're in the market for surnames, it wouldn't hurt to check your phone book as well.

To help you choose the very best name from all the ones you like, note your favorites and rate them on the baby name worksheets in the back of the book. If you happen to run across some terrific new names or variations that aren't included, please send them to Meadowbrook. That way the list can be updated to keep up with all the latest names.

Abbey, Abby familiar forms of Abigail.

Abigail (Hebrew) "father of joy." Biblical: one of the wives of King David.
Abagael, Abagail, Abbe, Abbey, Abbi, Abbie, Abby, Abbye, Abigael, Abigale, Gael, Gail, Gale, Gayel

Abra (Hebrew) "earth mother." A feminine form of Abraham.

Acacia (Greek) "thorny." The acacia tree symbolizes immortality and resurrection.
Cacia, Cacie, Casey, Casia, Kacie

Ada (Old English) "prosperous; happy." A short form of Adelaide.
Adah, Adan, Adda, Addi, Addia, Addie, Addy, Adey, Adi, Aida, Eada

Adalia (German, Spanish) "noble one."
Adal, Adala, Adali, Adalie

Adara (Greek) "beauty"; (Arabic) "virgin."

Adelaide (Old German) "noble; kind."
Addi, Addie, Addy, Adel, Adela, Adelaida, Adele, Adelheid, Adeline, Adelle, Aline, Del, Della, Delly, Edeline, Heidi

Adeline an English form of Adelaide.
Adaline, Adelina, Adelind, Adella

Adelle a French form of Adelaide.

Adena (Hebrew) "sensuous, voluptuous."
Adina, Dena, Dina

Adora (Latin) "beloved."
Adorée, Dora, Dori, Dorie, Dory

Adrienne (Latin) "dark; rich."
Adrea, Adria, Adrian, Adriana, Adriane, Adrianna, Adriena, Hadria

Africa (Celtic) "pleasant." Historical: twelfth-century queen of the Isle of Man.
Afrika, Africah, Afrikah, Affrica

Afton (Old English) "one from Afton."

Agatha (Greek) "good; kind."
Ag, Agace, Agata, Agathe, Aggi, Aggie, Aggy, Agueda

Agnes (Greek) "pure."
Ag, Aggi, Aggie, Agna, Agnella, Agnese, Agnesse, Agneta, Agnola, Aigneis, Annis, Ina, Ines, Inessa, Inez, Nessa, Nessi, Nessie, Nessy, Nesta, Nevsa, Neysa, Una, Ynes, Ynez

Aida an Italian form of Ada.

Aileen (Irish Gaelic) "light-bearer." An Irish form of Helen.
Aila, Ailee, Ailene, Ailey, Aili, Aleen, Alene, Aline, Eileen, Eleen, Elene, Ileana, Ileane, Ilene, Lena, Lina

Aimée a French form of Amy.

Ainsley (Scottish Gaelic) "from one's own meadow." Ainslee, Ainslie, Ansley

Aisha (African) "life." Asha, Ashia, Asia

Akili (Tanzanian) "wisdom." Akela, Akeyla, Akeylah

Alameda (Spanish) "poplar tree."

Alanna (Irish Gaelic) "fair, beautiful." A feminine form of Alan. See also Helen. Alaine, Alana, Alanah, Alane, Alayne, Alleen, Allene, Allina, Allyn, Lana, Lanna

Alberta (Old English) "noble, brilliant." A feminine form of Albert. Albertina, Albertine, Ali, Alli, Allie, Ally, Alverta, Auberta, Aubine, Bert, Berta, Berte, Berti, Bertie, Berty, Elberta, Elbertina, Elbertine

Alcina (Greek) "strong-minded." Alcine, Alcinia

Alethea (Greek) "truth." Alathia, Aletha, Alethia, Alithea, Alithia

Alexandra (Greek) "helper and defender of mankind." A feminine form of Alexander. Alejandra, Alejandrina, Alessandra, Alex, Alexa, Alexandrina, Alexina, Alexine, Alexis, Ali, Alix, Alla, Alli, Allie, Allix, Ally, Cesya, Elena, Lesya, Lexi, Lexie, Lexine, Lexy, Sande, Sandi, Sandie, Sandra, Sandy, Sandye, Sondra, Zandra

Alexis a form of Alexandra. Alexi, Alexia

Alfreda (Old English) "wise and diplomatic counselor." A feminine form of Alfred. Alfi, Alfie, Alfy, Elfie, Elfreda, Elfrida, Elfrieda, Elva, Freda, Freddie, Freddy, Frieda

Ali a short form of Alexandra; Alice.

Alice (Greek) "truth"; (Old German) "noble." See also Adelaide. Adelice, Ailis, Alecia, Aleece, Ali, Alica, Alicea, Alicia, Alika, Alikee, Alis, Alisa, Alisha, Alison, Alissa, Alla, Alli, Allie, Allison, Allsun, Allyce, Allys, Alyce, Alys, Alyse, Alysia, Alyss, Alyssa, Elissa, Ilysa, Ilyssa, Licha, Lissa, Lyssa

Alicia, Alisha English forms of Alice.

Alida (Greek) "beautifully dressed." Aleda, Alidia, Alyda, Leda, Lida

Alina (Slavic) "bright, beautiful." Aleen, Alena, Alene, Allene, Lina

Allegra (Latin) "exuberantly cheerful." Allie, Legra

Allison (Irish Gaelic) "little; truthful"; (Old German) "famous among the gods." An Irish form of Alice. Ali, Alie, Alisen, Alisha, Allson, Alissa, Alli, Allie, Allsun, Allyson, Alyson, Alyssa, Lissi, Lissie, Lissy

Alma (Arabic) "learned"; (Latin) "soul."

Almeda (Latin) "pressing toward the goal." Almeta

Almira (Arabic) "exalted." A feminine form of Elmer. Almeria, Almire, Elmira

Alta (Latin) "high."

Althea (Greek) "wholesome, healing." Thea

Alva (Spanish, Latin) "white; fair."

Alvina (Old English) "noble friend." A feminine form of Alvin.
Alvinia, Vina, Vinni, Vinnie, Vinny

Alyssa (Greek) "sane, logical; alyssum (a yellow flower)." See also Alice.
Alissa, Allissa, Alysa, Ilyssa, Lyssa

Ama (African) "born on Saturday."

Amabel (Latin) "lovable."
Amabelle, Belle

Amanda (Latin) "worthy of love."
Amandi, Amandie, Amandy, Manda, Mandi, Mandie, Mandy

Amara (Greek) "of eternal beauty."
Amargo, Mara

Amber (Old French) "amber."
Amberly, Ambur

Amelia (Old German) "hardworking." A form of Emily. See also Amy; Emma.
Amalea, Amalee, Amaleta, Amalia, Amalie, Amalita, Amélie, Amelina, Ameline, Amelita, Amy

Amity (Latin) "friendship."
Amitie

Amy (Latin) "beloved." See also Amelia; Emily.
Aimée, Amata, Ame, Ami, Amie, Amii, Amye, Esma, Esme

Anastasia (Greek) "of the Resurrection; of springtime."
Ana, Anastasie, Anastassia, Anestassia, Anstice, Asia, Stace, Stacey, Stacie, Stacy, Tasia

Anatola (Greek) "from the east."

Andrea (Latin) "womanly."
Aindrea, Andee, Anderea, Andra, Andrel, Andi, Andie, Andreana, Andrée, Andree, Andria, Andriana, Andy, Aundrea, Ondrea

Angela (Greek) "angel, messenger."
Ange, Angel, Angèle, Angelica, Angelika, Angelina, Angeline, Angelique, Angelita, Angelle, Angie, Angil, Angy, Gelya

Angelica a familiar form of Angela.

Angie a familiar form of Angela.

Anita a Spanish familiar form of Ann.
Anitra

Ann, Anne (Hebrew) "graceful." An English form of Hannah.
Ana, Anet, Anett, Anette, Ania, Anica, Anissa, Anita, Anitra, Anya, Anna, Annabel, Annabella, Annabelle, Annetta, Annette, Anni, Annice, Annie, Annis, Annora, Anny, Anuska, Anya, Hanna, Hannah, Hanni, Hannie, Hanny, Nan, Nana, Nance, Nancee, Nancey, Nanci, Nancie, Nancy, Nanete, Nanette, Nanice, Nanine, Nanni, Nannie, Nanny, Nanon, Netti, Nettie, Netty, Nina, Ninette, Ninon, Nita

Annabel a combination of Anna + Belle. See also Mabel.
Anabel, Anabella, Anabelle, Annabal, Annabell, Annabella, Annabelle

Annamaria a combination of Anna + Maria.
Annamarie, Annemarie, Annmaria

Annelise a combination of Anne + Lise.
Analiese, Analise, Anetta, Annaliese, Annalise, Anneliese, Annelise, Annissa

Annette a familiar form of Ann.
Anet, Anett, Anetta

Annissa a form of Annelise
Anissa

Anthea (Greek) "like a flower."
Anthe, Anthia, Thia

Antoinette (Latin) "priceless." A feminine form of Anthony.
Antonetta, Antonia, Antonie, Antonietta, Antonina, Netta, Netti, Nettie, Netty, Toinette, Toni, Tonia, Tonie, Tony, Tonye

Aphra (Hebrew) "female deer."
Afra

April (Latin) "opening."
Aprilette, Averil, Averyl, Avril

Ara (Arabic) "rainmaker."
Ari, Aria, Arria

Arabella (Latin) "beautiful altar."
Ara, Arabela, Arabele, Arabelle, Bel, Bella, Belle

Ardelle (Latin) "warmth, enthusiasm." See also Arden.
Arda, Ardeen, Ardelia, Ardelis, Ardella, Ardene, Ardine, Ardis, Ardra

Arden (Old English) "eagle-valley." Literary: Arden, in Shakespeare, is a romantic place of refuge.
Ardenia

Ardith (Hebrew) "flowering field."
Ardath, Ardis, Ardyce, Ardys, Ardyth, Aridatha, Datha

Arella (Hebrew) "angel messenger."
Arela

Aretha (Greek) "best."
Retha

Ariadne (Greek) "holy one." Mythological: the daughter of King Midas.
Ariana, Ariane, Arianie, Arianna

Ariel (Hebrew) "lioness of God."
Aeriela, Aeriel, Aeriell, Ariela, Ariella, Arielle

Arlene (Irish Gaelic) "pledge." A feminine form of Arlen.
Arlana, Arlee, Arleen, Arlen, Arlena, Arleta, Arlette, Arleyne, Arlie, Arliene, Arlina, Arlinda, Arline, Arluene, Arly, Arlyn, Arlyne, Lena, Lina

Ashley (Old English) "from the ash tree meadow."
Ashely, Ashla, Ashlee, Ashleigh, Ashlan, Ashlen, Ashley, Ashli, Ashly

Astrid (Scandinavian) "divine strength."
Astra

Astera, Asteria (Greek) "star."
Asta, Astra, Astraea, Astrea

Atalanta (Greek) "mighty adversary."
Atlanta, Atlante

Athalie (Hebrew) "the Lord is mighty."
Atalie, Athalee, Attalie

Athena (Greek) "wisdom." Mythological: the goddess of wisdom.
Athene

Aubrey (Old French) "blond ruler; elf ruler."
Aubree, Aubrette, Aubrie, Aubry

Audrey (Old English) "noble strength."
Audi, Audie, Audra, Audre, Audrie, Audry, Audrye

Augusta (Latin) "majestic."
A feminine form of August.
Auguste, Augustina, Augustine, Austin, Austina, Austine, Gus, Gussi, Gussie, Gussy, Gusta, Gusti, Gustie, Gusty, Tina

Aurelia (Latin) "golden."
Mythological: the goddess of the dawn.
Aura, Aurea, Aurel, Aurelea, Aurélie, Auria, Aurie, Aurilia, Aurora, Aurore, Ora, Oralee, Oralia, Oralie, Orel, Orelee, Orelia, Orelie

Aurora (Latin) "dawn." See also Aurelia.
Aurore, Ora, Rora, Rori, Rorie, Rory

Autumn (Latin) "autumn."
Autum

Ava (Latin) "birdlike." See also Avis.

Avery (Old French) "to confirm."
Averi

Avis (Old English) "refuge in battle." See also Ava.

Aviva (Hebrew) "springtime."
Avivah, Avrit, Viva

Bambi (Italian) "child."
Bambie, Bamby

Baptista (Latin) "baptizer."
Baptiste, Batista, Battista, Bautista

Bara, Barra (Hebrew) "to choose."
Bari

Barbara (Latin) "stranger."
Bab, Babara, Babb, Babbie, Babette, Babita, Babs, Barb, Barbe, Barbee, Barbette, Barbey, Barbi, Barbie, Barbra, Barby, Bobbee, Bobbi, Bobbie, Bobby, Bonni, Bonnie, Bonny

Barbie a familiar form of Barbara.

Barrie a feminine form of Barry.
Bari

Bathsheba (Hebrew) "daughter of the oath; seventh daughter." Biblical: one of the wives of King David.
Batsheva, Sheba

Bea, Bee short forms of Beatrice.

Beatrice (Latin) "bringer of joy."
Bea, Beatrisa, Beatrix, Bebe, Bee, Beitris, Trix, Trixi, Trixie, Trixy

Becky a familiar form of Rebecca.

Belicia (Spanish) "dedicated to God."
Bel

Belinda (Spanish) "beautiful"; Literary: a name coined by Alexander Pope in *The Rape of the Lock.*
Bel, Belle, Linda, Lindie, Lindy

Belle (French) "beautiful."
See also Isabel.
Belinda, Bell, Bella, Bellina, Belva, Belvia, Bill, Billi, Billie, Billy

Benita (Latin) "blessed." A feminine form of Benedict.
Bendite, Benedetta, Benedicta, Benedikta, Benetta, Benni, Bennie, Benny, Benoite, Binni, Binnie, Binny

Bernadine (French) "brave as a bear." A feminine form of Bernard.
Berna, Bernadene, Bernadette, Bernadina, Bernardina, Bernardine, Berneta, Bernetta, Bernette, Bernie, Bernita, Berny

Bernice (Greek) "bringer of victory."
Berenice, Bernelle, Bernetta, Bernette, Berni, Bernie, Berny, Bunni, Bunnie, Bunny, Nixie, Veronica, Veronika, Véronique

Bertha (Old German) "shining."
Berta, Berte, Berthe, Berti, Bertie, Bertina, Bertine, Berty, Bird, Birdie

Beryl (Greek) "beryl (a seagreen jewel)."
Berri, Berrie, Berry, Beryle

Bessie a familiar form of Elizabeth.
Bess

Beth (Hebrew) "house of God." A short form of names containing "beth": see Bethany; Elizabeth.

Bethany (Aramaic) "house of poverty." Biblical: a village near Jerusalem.
Beth, Bethena, Bethina

Betsy, Bette, Betty familiar forms of Elizabeth.

Beulah (Hebrew) "married." Biblical: the land of Beulah is a name for Israel.

Beverly (Old English) "from the beaver-meadow."
Bev, Beverle, Beverlee, Beverley, Beverlie, Bevvy, Buffy, Verlee, Verlie

Bianca an Italian form of Blanche.
Biancha

Bibi (Arabic) "lady."

Billie (Old English) "strong-willed." A familiar form of Wilhelmina. See also Belle.
Billi, Billy

Bina (African) "to dance"; (Hebrew) "wisdom, understanding."
Binah, Buna

Bird (English) "like a bird." See also Bertha.
Birdella, Birdie

Blaine (Irish Gaelic) "thin, lean."
Blane, Blayne

Blair (Scottish Gaelic) "dweller on the plain."
Blaire

Blake (Old English) "one with a swarthy complexion."
Blakelee, Blakeley

Blanche (Old French) "white; fair."
Bellanca, Bianca, Blanca, Blanch, Blanka, Blinni, Blinnie, Blinny

Bliss (Old English) "bliss, joy."
Blisse

Blondelle (French) "little fair one."
Blondell, Blondie, Blondy

Blossom (Old English) "flowerlike."

Blythe (Old English) "joyous."
Blithe

Bobbi, Bobbie, Bobby familiar forms of Roberta.

Bonita (Spanish) "pretty."

Bonnie, Bonny (Scottish-English) "beautiful, pretty." See also Barbara.
Bonnee, Bonni, Bonnibelle

Bradley (Old English) "from the broad meadow."
Bradlee, Bradleigh, Bradly

Brandy (Dutch) "brandy (a sweet after-dinner drink)."
Brandais, Brande, Brandea, Brandi, Brandice, Brandie, Bree

Brenda (Old English) "firebrand." A feminine form of Brandon; Brendan.
Bren, Brenn

Brenna (Irish Gaelic) "raven; raven-haired." A feminine form of Brendan.
Bren, Brenn

Brett (Irish Gaelic) "from Britain." See also Brittany.

Briana (Irish Gaelic) "strong." A feminine form of Brian.
Brana, Breana, Breanne, Breena, Bria, Brianna, Brianne, Brina, Briney, Brinn, Brinna, Briny, Bryana, Bryn, Bryna, Brynn, Brynne

Bridget (Irish Gaelic) "resolute strength."
Beret, Berget, Biddie, Biddy, Birgit, Birgitta, Bride, Bridgette, Bridie, Brietta, Brigid, Brigida, Brigit, Brigitta, Brigitte, Brita

Brier (French) "heather."
Brear

Brigitte a French form of Bridget.

Brina (Slavic) "protector." Also a feminine form of Brian.
Bryna, Brynna

Brittany (Latin) "from England." See also Brett.
Brit, Britney, Britni, Britt, Britta, Brittan, Brittaney, Brittani, Britteny, Brittnee, Brittney, Brittni

Bronwyn (Welsh) "white breast."
Bronnie, Bronny, Bronwen

Brooke (Old English) "from the brook." A feminine form of Brook.
Brook, Brooks

Brunhilda (Old German) "armored woman warrior."
Brunhilde, Hilda, Hilde

Bunny (English) "little rabbit." See also Bernice.
Bunni, Bunnie

Caitlin an Irish form of Catherine.
Catlee, Catlin, Kaitlin, Kaitlyn, Kaitlynn

Calandra (Greek) "lark."
Cal, Calandria, Calendre, Calley, Calli, Callie, Cally

Calida (Spanish) "warm, ardent."
Callida

Calla (Greek) "beautiful." A short form of Callista.
Cal, Calli, Callie, Cally

Callista (Greek) "most beautiful."
Calesta, Calista, Calla, Calli, Callie, Cally, Calysta, Kallista

Calypso (Greek) "concealer." Mythological: the sea nymph who kept Odysseus captive.

Camille (Latin) "young ceremonial attendant."
Cam, Camala, Camel, Cami, Camila, Camile, Camilla, Cammi, Cammie, Cammy, Milli, Millie, Milly

Candace, Candice (Greek) "glittering; flowing white." Historical: the name and title of the queens of ancient Ethiopia. See also Candida.
Candi, Candie, Candis, Candy, Kandace, Kandy

Candida (Latin) "pure white." See also Candace.
Candi, Candide, Candie, Candy

Candra (Latin) "luminescent."

Candy a familiar form of Candace; Candida.

Caprice (Italian) "fanciful."

Cara (Irish Gaelic) "friend"; (Latin) "dear."
Caralie, Carina, Carine, Carrie, Kara

Caresse (French) "beloved."

Cari (Turkish) "flows like water."

Carilla a feminine form of Charles.
Cari, Kari, Karilla

Carina (Latin) "keel." See also Karen.
Carena, Carin, Carine, Caryn, Karena, Karina, Karine

Carissa (Greek) "loving." See also Charity.
Caresa, Caressa, Carrissa, Charissa, Karisa, Karissa

Carita (Latin) "charity." See also Charity.
Caritta, Karita

Carla a short form of Caroline; a feminine form of Carl or Charles.
Karla

Carlie, Carly familiar forms of Caroline; Charlotte.
Carlee, Carley, Carli, Carlye, Karlee, Karli, Karlie, Karly

Carlotta an Italian form of Charlotte.

Carmel (Hebrew) "garden." Biblical: Mount Carmel was famed for the feats of Elijah.
Carma, Carmela, Carmelina, Carmelita, Lita

Carmen (Latin) "song"; (Spanish) "from Mount Carmel." Religious: the name honors *Santa Maria del Carmen*, "Mary of Mount Carmel."
Carma, Carmelina, Carmelita, Carmencita, Carmina, Carmine, Carmita, Charmaine, Karmen

Carol (Latin) "strong; womanly"; (Old French) "song of joy." A feminine form of Carl; Charles.
Carey, Cari, Carla, Carleen, Carlen, Carlene, Carley, Carlin, Carlina, Carline, Carlita, Carlota, Carlotta, Carly, Carlyn, Carlynn, Carlynne, Caro, Carola, Carole, Carolin, Carolina, Caroline, Carolyn, Carolynn, Carolynne, Carri, Carrie, Carroll, Carry, Cary, Caryl, Charla, Charleen, Charlena, Charlene, Charlotta, Charmain, Charmaine, Charmian, Charmion, Charyl, Cheryl, Cherlyn, Karel, Kari, Karla, Karleen, Karlen, Karlene, Karlotta, Karlotte, Karole, Karolina, Karoly, Karyl, Kerril, Lola, Loleta, Lolita, Lotta, Lotte, Lotti, Lottie, Sharleen, Sharlene, Sharline, Sharyl, Sherrie, Sherry, Sherye, Sheryl

Caroline, Carolyn (Latin) "little and womanly." Modern familiar forms of Carol. A feminine form of Carl; Charles. See also Charlotte.
Carla, Carleen, Carlen, Carlene, Carley, Carlin, Carlina, Carline, Carlita, Carlota, Carlotta, Carly, Carlyn, Carlynn, Carlynne, Carol, Carola, Carole, Carolin, Carolina, Carolyne, Carolynn, Carolynne, Carri, Carrie, Carroll, Cary, Charla, Charleen, Charlena, Charlene, Karla, Karleen, Karlen, Karlene, Karolina, Karolyn

Carrie a familiar form of Carol; Caroline.
Carey, Cari, Carie, Cary, Carree, Carri, Carry, Kari, Karrie

Casey (Irish Gaelic) "brave."
Casi, Casie, Kacey, Kacie, Kacy, Kasey, Kaycee

Cassandra (Greek) "helper of men; disbelieved by men." Mythological: a prophetess of ancient Greece.
Casandra, Cass, Cassandre, Cassandry, Cassaundra, Cassi, Cassie, Cassondra, Cassy, Kassandra, Sandi, Sandie, Sandy, Saundra, Sondra,

Cassie a short form of Cassandra; Catherine.
Cassey, Cassi, Kassey, Kassi

Catherine (Greek) "pure." An English form of Katherine.
Caitlin, Caitrin, Caren, Cari, Carin, Caron, Caryn, Cass, Cassi, Cassie, Cassy, Catarina, Cate, Caterina, Catha, Catharina, Catharine, Cathe, Cathee, Catherin, Catherina, Cathi, Cathie, Cathleen, Cathlene, Cathyleen, Cathrine, Cathryn, Cathy, Cati, Catie, Catina, Catlaina, Catrina, Catriona, Caty, Caye, Ekaterina

Cathi, Cathy short forms of Catherine.

Cecilia (Latin) "blind." A feminine form of Cecil.
Cacilia, Cacilie, Cecil, Cecile, Ceciley, Cecily, Ceil, Cele, Celia, Celie, Cicely, Cicily, Ciel, Cilka, Cissie, Cissy, Kikelia, Sile, Sileas, Sisely, Sisile, Sissie, Sissy

Celeste (Latin) "heavenly."
Cele, Celesta, Celestia, Celestina, Celestine, Celestyn, Celestyna, Celia, Celie, Celina, Celinda, Celine, Celinka, Celisse, Celka, Selestina

Celia a short form of Cecilia.

Chanda (Sanskrit) "the great goddess." Mythological: the name assumed by Devi, the greatest goddess.
Shanda

Chandra (Sanskrit) "moonlike." Mythological: one of the names of the great Hindu goddess Shakti.
Shandra

Chantal a French form of the Latin *cantus,* meaning, "a song."
Chandal, Chantalle

Charity (Latin) "charity, brotherly love."
Carissa, Carita, Charis, Charissa, Charita, Cherri, Cherry, Sharity

Charlene a familiar form of Caroline; Charlotte.
Charleen

Charlotte (French) "little and womanly." A French form of Carol. A feminine form of Charles. See also Caroline.
Carla, Carleen, Carlene, Carline, Carlota, Carlotta, Carly, Chara, Charil, Charla, Charleen, Charlene, Charline, Charlotta, Charmain, Charmaine, Charmian, Charmion, Charo, Charyl, Cherlyn, Cheryl, Karla, Karleen, Karlene, Karlotta, Karlotte, Lola, Loleta, Lolita, Lotta, Lotte, Lotti, Lottie, Sharleen, Sharlene, Sharline, Sharyl, Sherrie, Sherry, Sherye, Sheryl

Charmaine a French familiar form of Carmen; Charlotte.
Charmain, Charmane, Charmian, Charmion

Chastity (Latin) "purity."

Chelsea (Old English) "a port of ships."
Chelsae, Chelsey, Chelsie, Chelsy, Cheslie

Cher (French) "beloved."
Cherice, Chere, Cherey, Cheri, Chérie, Cherice, Cherise, Cherish, Chery, Cherye, Sher, Sherry, Sherye

Chérie a familiar form of Cher.

Cherry (Old French) "cherrylike." A familiar form of Charity.
Cherey, Cherida, Cherri, Cherrita

Cheryl a familiar form of Charlotte. See also Shirley.
Charyl, Cherianne, Cherilyn, Cherilynn

Chesna (Slavic) "peaceful."
Chessa, Chessy

Chiquita (Spanish) "little one."
Chickie, Chicky

Chloe (Greek) "young grass." Mythological: the goddess of green grain.
Chloë, Clo, Cloe

Chloris (Greek) "pale." Mythological: the only daughter of Niobe to escape the vengeful arrows of Apollo and Diana.
Cloris

Chris, Chrissy short forms of Christine.

Christabel (Latin-French) "beautiful Christian."
Christabella, Cristabel

Christina, Cristina short forms of Christine.

Christine (Greek) "Christian; anointed."
Cairistiona, Cristen, Crystie, Chris, Chrissie, Chrissy, Christa, Christan, Christel, Christean, Christen, Christi, Christian, Christiana, Christiane, Christie, Christin, Christina, Christy, Christye, Christyna, Chrysa, Chrystal, Chryste, Cris, Crissie, Crissy, Crista, Cristi, Cristie, Cristin, Cristina, Cristine, Cristiona, Cristy, Crystal, Kirsten, Kirstin, Kris, Krissie, Krissy, Krista, Kristel, Kristen, Kristi, Kristie, Kristin, Kristina, Kristy, Krysta, Krystyna, Tina

Christy a short form of Christina; Christine.

Cicely an English form of Cecilia.

Cinderella (French) "little one of the ashes." Literary: a name from the fairy tale.
Cindy, Ella

Cindy a short form of Cinderella; Cynthia; Lucinda.

Claire a French form of Clara.

Clara (Greek) "clear, bright."
Chiarra, Clair, Claire, Clarabelle, Clare, Claresta, Clareta, Claretta, Clarette, Clarey, Clari, Clarice, Clarie, Clarinda, Clarine, Clarissa, Clarita, Clary, Klara, Klarika, Klarrisa

Clarissa (Latin-Greek) "most brilliant." A modern form of Clara.
Clerissa

Claudia (Latin) "lame." A feminine form of Claude.
Claude, Claudelle, Clauddetta, Claudette, Claudie, Claudina, Claudine, Gladys

Clea Literary: a name perhaps coined by Lawrence Durrell in *The Alexandria Quartet*. See also Cleo; Clio.

Clementine (Greek) "mercy."
Clem, Clemence, Clementia, Clementina, Clemmie, Clemmy

Cleo (Greek) "famous." A short form of Cleopatra, name of the great Egyptian queen.
Clea

Clio (Greek) "announcer." Mythological: the Greek muse of history.

Clover (Old English) "clover blossom."

Cody (Old English) "a cushion."
Codee, Codi, Codie

Colette (Greek-French) "victorious in battle." A familiar form of Nicole.
Collete, Coletta, Collette

Colleen (Irish Gaelic) "girl."
Coleen, Colene, Collie, Colline, Colly

Concepcion (Latin) "conception, generation."
Chita, Concha, Conchita

Concordia (Latin) "harmony." Mythological: the goddess governing the peace after war.

Connie a short form of Constance.

Constance (Latin) "constancy, firmness."
Con, Conni, Connie, Conny, Constancia, Constancy, Constanta, Constantia, Constantina, Constantine, Costanza, Konstance, Konstanze

Consuelo (Spanish) "consolation." Religious: the name honors *Santa Maria del Consuelo*, "Mary of Consolation."
Consolata, Consuela

Cora a modern form of Kora.
Corabel, Corabella, Corabelle, Corella, Corena, Corenda, Corene, Coretta, Corette, Corey, Cori, Corie, Corilla, Corina, Corinna, Corinne, Coriss, Corissa, Corrina, Corrine, Corry

Coral (Latin) "coral."
Coralie, Coraline, Koral, Koralie

Cordelia (Welsh) "jewel of the sea."
Cordélie, Cordey, Cordi, Cordie, Cordula, Cordy, Delia, Della, Kordula

Coretta a familiar form of Cora.

Corey (Irish Gaelic) "from the hollow."
Cory, Cori, Corie, Correy, Corri, Corrie, Corry, Kori, Korrie, Korry

Corinna, Corinne familiar forms of Cora.
Coreen, Corine, Correna, Corrianne, Corrinne

Corliss (Old English) "cheerful, good-hearted."
Corly

Cornelia (Latin) "yellow; horn-colored." A feminine form of Cornelius.
Cornela, Cornélie, Cornelle, Cornie, Corny, Neely, Nelia, Nelie, Nell, Nellie, Nelly

Courtney (Old English) "from the court."
Cortney, Courtenay, Courtnay, Korney

Crissy, Cristy short forms of Christine.

Crystal (Latin) "clear as crystal." See also Christine.
Cristal, Crysta, Christal, Christalle, Chrystal, Krystal

Cybil a form of Sibyl.

Cynthia (Greek) "moon." Mythological: another name for the moon goddess.
Cinda, Cindee, Cindi, Cindie, Cindy, Cynde, Cyndia, Cyndie, Cynthea, Cynthie, Cynthy, Kynthia, Sindee

Cyrilla (Latin) "lordly." A feminine form of Cyril.
Ciri, Cirilla

Dacey (Irish Gaelic) "southerner."
Dacia, Dacie, Dacy, Dasi, Dasie

Dagmar (Old German) "glorious day."

Dahlia (Scandinavian) "from the valley."
Dalia

Daisy (Old English) "eye of the day; daisy flower."
Daisey, Daisi, Daisie

Dale (Old English) "from the valley."
Dael, Daile, Dayle

Dalenna a familiar form of Madeline.

Dalila (African) "gentle." See also Delilah.
Lila

Dallas (Irish Gaelic) "wise."

Damara (Greek) "gentle girl."
Damaris, Mara, Maris

Damita (Spanish) "little noble lady."

Dana (Scandinavian) "from Denmark."
Dayna, Tana

Danae (Greek). Mythological: the mother of Perseus.
Dee, Denae, Dene

Danica (Slavic) "the morning star."
Danika

Danielle (Hebrew) "judged by God." A feminine form of Daniel.
Danella, Danelle, Danette, Dani, Danice, Daniela, Daniele, Daniella, Danila, Danit, Danita, Danna, Danni, Dannie, Danny, Dannye, Danya, Danyelle

Daphne (Greek) "laurel tree."
Daffi, Daffie, Daffy, Daphna

Dara (Hebrew) "compassion."
Darda, Darya

Darby (Irish Gaelic) "free man"; (Old Norse) "from the deer estate."
Darb, Darbie

Darcie, Darcy (Irish Gaelic) "dark."
Darcee, Darcey, Darcie, Darice, Darsey

Daria (Greek) "queenly." A feminine form of Darius.
Dari

Darlene (Old French) "little darling."
Dareen, Darelle, Darla, Darleen, Darline, Darlleen, Darrelle, Darryl, Daryl

Daron (Irish Gaelic) "great." A feminine form of Darren.

Davita (Hebrew) "beloved." A feminine form of David.
Daveen, Daveta, Davida, Davina, Davine, Devina, Veda, Vida, Vita, Vitia

Dawn (Old English) "dawn."

Deanna a familiar form of Dena; Diana. A feminine form of Dean.
Deana, Deanna, Deanne

Deborah (Hebrew) "bee." Biblical: a great Hebrew prophetess.
Deb, Debi, Debbee, Debbi, Debbie, Debby, Debi, Debor, Debora, Debra, Devora

Debbi, Debbie, Debby short forms of Deborah.

Dee (Welsh) "black, dark." A short form of Deirdre; Delia; Diana.
Dede, Dedie, Dee Dee, DeeAnn, Didi

Deirdre (Irish Gaelic) "sorrow; complete wanderer."
Dede, Dedra, Dee, Dee Dee, Deerdre, Deidre, Didi, Dierdre

Delaney (Irish Gaelic) "descendent of the challenger."
Delaney, Delanie

Delia (Greek) "visible; from Delos." A short form of Cordelia. Mythological: a name for the moon goddess. See also Adelaide.
Dee, Dede, Dee Dee, Dehlia, Dela, Delinda, Della, Didi

Delilah (Hebrew) "brooding." Biblical: the companion of Samson.
Dalila, Delila, Lila, Lilah

Della a familiar form of Adelaide; Delia.

Delphine (Greek) "calmness."
Delfeena, Delfine, Delphina, Delphinia

Demetria (Greek) "belonging to Demeter (goddess of harvest)."
Demeter, Demetra, Demetris

Dena (Hebrew) "vindicated"; (Old English) "from the valley." A feminine form of Dean. See also Diana; Dinah.
Deana, Deane, Deanna, Deena, Deeyn, Dene, Denna, Denni, Dina

Denise (French) "adherent of Dionysus (god of wine)." A feminine form of Dennis.
Deni, Denice, Denni, Dennie, Denny, Denys, Denyse, Dinnie, Dinny

Desiree (French) "longed-for."
Desirae, Désirée, Desiri

Destinee (Old French) "destiny."

Deva (Sanskrit) "divine." Mythological: a name for the moon goddess.
Devi

Devin (Irish Gaelic) "poet."
Devan, Devinne

Devonna (Old English) "defender (of Devonshire)."
Devon, Devondra, Devonne

Diana (Latin) "divine." Mythological: the goddess of the hunt, the moon, and fertility.
Deana, Deane, Deanna, Deanne, Dede, Dee, Dee Dee, Dena, Di, Diahann, Dian, Diandra, Diane, Dianna, Dianne, Didi, Dyan, Dyana, Dyane, Dyann, Dyanna, Dyanne

Diane a form of Diana.

Dianthe (Greek) "divine flower."
Diandre, Diantha

Dinah (Hebrew) "vindicated." Biblical: a daughter of Jacob and Leah. See also Dena; Diana.
Dina, Dyna, Dynah

Dionne (Greek) "divine queen." Mythological: the mother of Aphrodite.
Deonne, Dion, Dione, Dionis

Dixie (French) "ten, tenth." A name from a term for the American South: "girl born in Dixie."
Dix

Dodie (Hebrew) "beloved." A familiar form of Dora.
Dodi, Dody

Dolly a familiar form of Dorothy.
Dolley, Dollie

Dolores (Spanish) "sorrows." Religious: the name honors Santa Maria de los Dolores, "Mary of the Sorrows."
Delora, Delores, Deloria, Deloris, Dolorita, Doloritas, Lola, Lolita

Dominique (French-Latin) "belonging to God." A feminine form of Dominic.
Domeniga, Dominga, Domini, Dominica

Donna (Latin-Italian) "lady."
Doña, Donella, Donelle, Donetta, Donia, Donica, Donielle, Donnell, Donni, Donnie, Donny, Ladonna

Dora (Greek) "gift." See also Doris; Dorothy.
Dode, Dodi, Dodie, Dody, Doralia, Doralin, Doralyn, Doralynn, Doralynne, Dore, Doreen, Dorelia, Dorella, Dorelle, Dorena, Dorene, Doretta, Dorette, Dorey, Dori, Dorie, Dorita, Doro, Dorree, Dory

Doreen (Irish Gaelic) "sullen." An Irish familiar form of Dora.
Dorene, Dorine

Dori, Dory familiar forms of Dora; Doria; Doris; Dorothy.

Doria (Greek) "Dorian." See also Doris.
Dori, Dorian, Dorice, Dory, Dorree

Doris (Greek) "from the sea." Mythological: the wife of Nereus and mother of the Nereids (sea nymphs). See also Dora; Dorothy.
Dori, Doria, Dorice, Dorisa, Dorise, Dorita, Dorri, Dorrie, Dorris, Dorry, Dory

Dorothy (Greek) "gift of God." See also Dora; Doris.
Dasha, Dasya, Dode, Dody, Doe, Doll, Dolley, Dolli, Dollie, Dolly, Dora, Dori, Dorlisa, Doro, Dorolice, Dorotea, Doroteya, Dorothea, Dorothée, Dorthea, Dorthy, Dory, Dosi, Dot, Dotti, Dottie, Dotty

Dottie, Dotty familiar forms of Dorothy.

Drusilla (Latin) "descendant of Drusus, the strong one."
Drew, Dru, Druci, Drucie, Drucill, Drucy, Drusi, Drusie, Drusy

Dulcie (Latin) "sweetness."
Delcina, Delcine, Dulce, Dulcea, Dulci, Dulcia, Dulciana, Dulcine, Dulcinea, Dulcy, Dulsea

Dusty a feminine form of Dustin.

Dylana a feminine form of Dylan.
Dylane

Earla a feminine form of Earl.
Earleen, Earlene, Erlene, Erlina, Erline

Eartha (Old English) "of the earth."
Erda, Ertha, Herta, Hertha

Easter (Old English) "Easter time." Religious: a name for a child born at Easter.

Ebony (Greek) "a hard, dark wood."
Ebonee

Echo (Greek) "repeated voice." Mythological: the nymph who pined for the love of Narcissus until only her voice remained.

Eden (Babylonian) "a plain"; (Hebrew) "delight." Biblical: the earthly paradise.
Edin

Edie a short form of Edith.

Edith (Old English) "rich gift."
Dita, Eadith, Eadie, Eda, Ede, Edi, Edie, Edita, Editha, Edithe, Ediva, Edy, Edyth, Edythe, Eyde, Eydie

Edna (Hebrew) "rejuvenation." Apocryphal: the wife of Enoch.
Eddi, Eddie, Eddy

Edwina (Old English) "prosperous friend." A feminine form of Edwin.
Edina, Edwyna, Win, Wina

Effie (Greek) "well spoken of."
Effy, Eppie, Euphemia, Euphémie

Eileen an Irish form of Helen.

Elaine a French form of Helen.
Elaina, Elana, Elane, Elayne, Lainey, Layney

Eldora (Spanish) "golden, gilded." A feminine form of Eldorado.
Eldoree, Eldoria

Eleanor (Greek) "light." A form of Helen.
Eleanora, Eleanore, Elenore, Elénore, Eleonore, Elianora, Elianore, Elinor, Elinore, Ella, Elladine, Elle, Ellen, Ellene, Elli, Ellie, Elly, Ellyn, Elna, Elnora, Elnore, Elora, Elyn, Leanor, Leanora, Lena, Lenora, Lenore, Leonora, Leonore, Leora, Nell, Nellie, Nelly, Nora

Electra (Greek) "shining, brilliant."

Elise a French familiar form of Elizabeth. See also Elysia.

Elissa a familiar form of Alice; Elizabeth.
Alyssa, Elyssa, Ellissa, Lissie, Lissy

Elita (Old French-Latin) "chosen."
Lita

Eliza a short form of Elizabeth.

Elizabeth (Hebrew) "oath of God." Biblical: the mother of John the Baptist.
Belita, Belle, Bess, Bessie, Bessy, Beth, Betsey, Betsy, Betta, Bette, Betti, Bettina, Bettine, Betty, Ealasaid, Eilis, Elisa, Elisabet, Elisabeth, Elisabetta, Elise, Elissa, Eliza, Elizabet, Elsa, Elsbeth, Else, Elsey, Elsi, Elsie, Elspet, Elspeth, Elsy, Elyse, Helsa, Isabel, Lib, Libbey, Libbi, Libbie, Libby, Lisa, Lisabeth, Lisbeth, Lise, Lisette, Lissa, Lissie, Lissy, Liz, Liza, Lizabeth, Lizbeth, Lizzie, Lizzy, Lusa, Ysabel

Elke a familiar form of Alice or Alexandra.
Elka, Ilka

Ella (Old English) "elf; beautiful fairy woman."
Ellette, Elli, Ellie, Elly

Ellen an English form of Helen.
Ellene, Ellie, Elly, Ellyn

Ellie, Elly short forms of Eleanor; Ella; Ellen.

Elmina (Old German) "awe-inspiring fame"; (Old English) "tree."

Eloise a French form of Louise.
Eloisa, Héloïse

Elsa (Old German) "noble." A familiar form of Elizabeth.
Else, Elsie, Elsy, Ilsa, Ilse

Elsie, Elsy forms of Elsa; Elizabeth.

Elvira (German-Spanish) "elf-counsel; excelling."
Elva, Elvera, Elvina, Elwira, Lira

Elysia (Latin) "sweetly blissful." Mythological: Elysium was the dwelling place of happy souls. See also Elise.
Elicia, Elise, Elisha, Elyse, Elysha, Ilise, Ilysa, Ilyse

Emily (Old German) "industrious"; (Latin) "flatterer." A form of Amelia; a feminine form of Emil. See also Amy; Emma.
Aimil, Amalea, Amalia, Amalie, Amelia, Amélie, Ameline, Amelita, Amy, Eimile, Em, Emalee, Emalia, Emelda, Emelia, Emelina, Emeline, Emelita, Emelyne, Emera, Emilee, Emili, Emilia, Emilie, Emiline, Emlyn, Emlynn, Emlynne, Emmalee, Emmaline, Emmalyn, Emmalynn, Emmalynne, Emmey, Emmi, Emmie, Emmy, Emmye, Emyle, Emylee, Milka

Emma (Old German) "universal; nurse." A short form of Emily. See also Amelia; Amy.
Em, Ema, Emelina, Emeline, Emelyne, Emmaline, Emmalyn, Emmalynn, Emmalynne, Emmi, Emmie, Emmy, Emmye

Enid (Welsh) "purity; woodlark."

Erica (Scandinavian) "everpowerful." A feminine form of Eric.
Aarika, Enrica, Enrika, Ericha, Ericka, Erika, Ricki, Rickie, Ricky, Rikki

Erin (Irish Gaelic) "peace." Literary: another name for Ireland.
Aaren, Aryn, Eran, Erina, Erinn, Erinna, Eryn

Erma a form of Irma. A short form of Hermione.
Ermina, Erminia, Erminie

Ermine (Latin) "regal."
Ermin, Erminia

Ernestine (Old English) "earnest." A feminine form of Ernest.
Erna, Ernaline, Ernesta

Esmeralda (Spanish, Greek) "the emerald."
Esma, Esmaria, Esme, Ezmeralda

Estelle (Old French) "star." See also Esther; Stella.
Estel, Estele, Estell, Estella, Estrella, Estrellita, Stella

Esther (Persian) "star." Biblical: Persian name of the Jewish captive Hadassah, whom Ahasuerus made his queen. See also Estelle; Stella.
Essa, Essie, Essy, Esta, Ester, Etti, Ettie, Etty, Hester, Hesther, Hettie, Hetty

Etana (Hebrew) "strong." A feminine form of Ethan.

Ethel (Old English) "noble."
Ethelda, Ethelin, Etheline, Ethelyn, Ethyl

Etta (Old German) "little." A familiar form of Henrietta.
Etty

Eudora (Greek) "honored gift."
Dora

Eugenia (Greek) "wellborn." A feminine form of Eugene.
Eugénie, Gene, Genia

Eulalia (French, Greek) "fair of speech."
Eula, Eulalee, Eulalie

Eunice (Greek) "happy victory." Biblical: the mother of Timothy.

Eurydice (Greek) "broad." Mythological: wife of Orpheus.
Euridice

Eustacia (Latin) "fruitful; tranquil." A feminine form of Eustace.
Stacey, Stacia, Stacie, Stacy

Eva a short form of Evangeline; a form of Eve.

Evadne (Greek) "fortunate."
Evanne

Evangeline (Greek) "bearer of good tidings."
Eva, Evangelia, Evangelina, Eve

Evania (Greek) "tranquil, untroubled."
Evanne

Eve (Hebrew) "life." Biblical: the wife of Adam. See also Evelyn; Yvonne.
Eba, Ebba, Eva, Evaleen, Evelina, Eveline, Evelyn, Evey, Evie, Evita, Evonne, Evvie, Evvy, Evy

Evelyn perhaps a combination of Eve and Helen.
Aveline, Eveleen

Evetta (African) "a hunt."
Evette

Faith (Middle English) "fidelity." See also Fay; Fidelity.
Fae, Fay, Faye, Fayth, Faythe

Faline (Latin) "catlike."

Fallon (Irish Gaelic) "grandchild of the ruler."

Fanny a familiar form of Frances.
Fan, Fanni, Fannie

Farrah (Middle English) "beautiful; pleasant."
Fara, Farah, Farand, Farra, Farrand, Fayre

Fatima (Arabic) "unknown." Historical: the daughter of Muhammad.
Fatimah, Fatma

Fawn (Old French) "young deer."
Faina, Fanya, Faun, Faunia, Fawne, Fawnia

Fay (Old French) "fairy; elf." See also Faith.
Fae, Faye, Fayette, Fayina

Felicia (Latin) "happy." A feminine form of Felix.
Felecia, Felice, Felicidad, Félicie, Felicity, Félise, Felisha, Felita, Feliza

Fern (Old English) "fern." A short form of Fernanda.
Ferne

Fernanda (Old German) "adventurer." A feminine form of Ferdinand.
Ferdinanda, Ferdinande, Fern, Fernande, Fernandina

Fidelity (Latin) "faithfulness." See also Faith.
Fidela, Fidelia

Fifi a French familiar form of Josephine.
Fifine

Fiona (Irish Gaelic) "fair."
Fionna

Fionnula (Irish Gaelic) "white-shouldered."
Fenella, Finella

Flannery (Old French) "a flat piece of metal."
Flan, Flann, Flanna

Flavia (Latin) "blonde, yellow-haired."

Flora (Latin) "flower." A short form of Florence.
Fiora, Fiore, Fleur, Flo, Flor, Flore, Florella, Floria, Florie, Floris, Florri, Florrie, Florry

Florence (Latin) "blooming; prosperous."
Fiorenza, Flo, Flor, Flora, Florance, Flore, Florencia, Florentia, Florenza, Flori, Floria, Florida, Florie, Florina, Florinda, Florine, Floris, Florri, Florrie, Florry, Floss, Flossi, Flossie, Flossy

Florida (Latin) "flowery, blooming." A Spanish form of Florence.
Floridia

Fonda (Spanish, Latin) "the profound."
Fondea

Fran, Frannie short forms of Frances.

Frances (Latin) "free; from France." A feminine form of Francis.
Fan, Fanchette, Fanchon, Fancie, Fancy, Fanechka, Fania, Fanni, Fannie, Fanny, Fanya, Fran, Francesca, Franci, Francie, Francine, Francisca, Franciska, Françoise, Francyne, Frank, Frankie, Franky, Franni, Frannie, Franny

Francine a French familiar form of Frances.

Françoise a French form of Frances.

Freda (Old German) "peaceful." A short form of Frederica.
Frayda, Fredella, Freida, Frieda

Frederica (Old German) "peaceful ruler." A feminine form of Frederick.
Farica, Federica, Fred, Freddi, Freddie, Freddy, Fredericka, Frédérique, Fredia, Fredra, Fredrika, Friederike, Rica, Ricki, Rickie, Ricky, Rikki

Freya (Scandinavian) "noble woman; the goddess Freya."
Fraya

Frieda a form of Freda.

Fulvia (Latin) "the blonde."

Gabrielle (Hebrew) "God is my strength." A feminine form of Gabriel.
Gabbey, Gabbi, Gabbie, Gabey, Gabi, Gabie, Gabriel, Gabriela, Gabriell, Gabriella, Gabriellia, Gabrila, Gaby, Gavra, Gavrielle

Gail (Old English) "gay, lively." A short form of Abigail. A form of Gay.
Gael, Gale, Gayla, Gayle, Gayleen, Gaylene

Galina a Russian form of Helen.

Garland (Old French) "garland."

Garnet (Middle English) "garnet (a dark red gem)." **Garnette**

Gavrila (Hebrew) "heroine; strong." A feminine form of Gabriel. **Gavriella, Gavrielle, Gavrilla**

Gay (Old French) "merry." A form of Gail. See also Abigail. **Gae, Gaye**

Gemini (Greek) "twin." **Gemina**

Gemma (Latin, Italian) "jewel, precious stone." **Jemma**

Gene a form of Jean.

Geneva (Old French) "juniper tree." A short form of Genevieve. See also Jennifer. **Gena, Genevra, Janeva**

Genevieve (Old German-French) "white wave." A form of Guinevere. See also Jennifer. **Gena, Geneva, Geneviève, Genevra, Gennie, Genny, Genovera, Gina, Janeva, Jennie, Jenny**

Georgeanne a familiar form of Georgia. **Georgeanna, Georgetta, Georgiana, Georgianna, Georgianne**

Georgia (Latin) "farmer." A feminine form of George. **George, Georgeanna, Georgeanne, Georgena, Georgetta, Georgette, Georgiana, Georgianna, Georgianne, Georgie, Georgina, Georgine, Giorgia**

Geraldine (Old German-French) "spear-mighty." A feminine form of Gerald. **Deena, Dina, Geralda, Geraldina, Géraldine, Gerhardine, Geri, Gerianna, Gerianne, Gerri, Gerrie, Gerrilee, Gerry, Giralda, Jeralee, Jere, Jeri, Jerrie, Jerry**

Geri, Gerri, Gerrie, Gerry short forms of Geraldine.

Germaine (French) "German." **Germain, Germana, Jermaine**

Gertrude (Old German) "spear strength; warrior woman." **Gerda, Gert, Gerta, Gerti, Gertie, Gertrud, Gertruda, Gertrudis, Gerty, Trude, Trudi, Trudie, Trudy**

Gigi a familiar form of Gilberte.

Gilberte (Old German) "brilliant pledge." A feminine form of Gilbert. **Berta, Berte, Berti, Bertie, Berty, Gigi, Gilberta, Gilbertina, Gilbertine, Gill, Gilli, Gillie, Gilly**

Gilda (Old English) "covered with gold." See also Golda.

Gina a familiar form of Angelina; Regina. **Jena**

Ginger (Latin) "ginger (the flower or the spice)." A familiar form of Virginia.

Ginny a familiar form of Virginia.

Giselle (Old German) "pledge; hostage." **Gisela, Gisele, Gisella, Gizela**

Gladys (Celtic) "princess"; (Latin) "small sword; gladiolus flower." A Welsh form of Claudia. **Glad, Gladi, Gleda**

Glenda a form of Glenna.

Glenna (Irish Gaelic) "from the valley or glen." A feminine form of Glenn.
Glenda, Glenine, Glen, Glenn, Glennie, Glennis, Glyn, Glynis, Glynnis

Gloria (Latin) "glory."
Glori, Gloriana, Gloriane, Glory

Glynis a Welsh form of Glenna.
Glynnis

Golda (Old English) "gold." See also Gilda.
Goldarina, Goldi, Goldia, Goldie, Goldina, Goldy

Grace (Latin) "graceful."
Engracia, Gracia, Gracie, Grata, Gratia, Gratiana, Gray, Grayce, Grazia

Greer a Scottish short feminine form of Gregor (from Gregory).
Grier

Greta a German short form of Margaret.
Gretchen, Grete, Gretel, Gretna, Gretta

Gretchen a German form of Margaret.

Griselda (Old German) "gray woman warrior."
Griseldis, Grishilda, Grishilde, Grissel, Grizel, Grizelda, Selda, Zelda

Guadalupe (Arabic) "river of black stones."
Lupe, Lupita

Gudrun (Scandinavian) "war; close friend."
Gudren, Gudrin

Guinevere (Welsh) "white, fair; white wave." Literary: the wife of King Arthur. See also Gwendolyn.
Freddi, Freddie, Freddy, Fredi, Gaynor, Genevieve, Genna, Genni, Gennie, Gennifer, Genny, Ginevra, Guenevere, Guenna, Guinna, Gwen, Gwenora, Gwenore, Janifer, Jen, Jenifer, Jennee, Jenni, Jennie, Jennifer, Jenny, Ona, Oona, Una, Winifred, Winni, Winnie, Winny

Gwen a short form of Guinevere; Gwendolyn.

Gwendolyn (Welsh) "white; white-browed." Literary: the wife of Merlin in Arthurian legend. See also Genevieve; Guinevere; Jennifer; Wanda.
Guendolen, Guenna, Gwen, Gwendolen, Gwendolin, Gwenette, Gwenni, Gwennie, Gwenny, Gwyn, Gwyneth, Gwynne, Wendi, Wendie, Wendy, Wynne

Gwyneth (Welsh) "white; blessed." A form of Gwendolyn. See also Guinevere.
Gwynne, Winnie, Winny, Wynne, Wynnie, Wynny

Gypsy (Old English) "wanderer."
Gipsy

Haley (Scandinavian) "hero."
Hailee, Haily, Haleigh, Halie, Hally, Hayley

Halla (African) "unexpected gift."

Hallie (Greek) "thinking of the sea."
Halette, Hali, Halimeda, Halley, Halli, Hally

Halona (North American Indian) "fortunate."

Hana (Japanese) "flower." A German form of Hannah.
Hanae, Hanako

Hannah (Hebrew) "graceful." A Hebrew form of Ann. Biblical: the mother of Samuel.
Hana, Hanna, Hanni, Hannie, Hanny, Honna

Happy (English) "happy."

Harley (Old English) "from the long field."
Harlene, Harli, Harlie

Harmony (Latin) "harmony."
Harmonia, Harmonie

Harriet (Old French) "ruler of the home." A feminine form of Harry. See also Henrietta.
Harri, Harrie, Harrietta, Harriette, Harriot, Harriott, Hatti, Hattie, Hatty

Hattie, Hatty familiar forms of Harriet; Henrietta.

Hazel (Old English) "hazelnut tree; commanding authority."
Aveline

Heather (Middle English) "flowering heather."
Heath

Hedda (Old German) "strife."
Heda, Hedi, Heddi, Heddie, Hedvige, Hedwig, Hedwiga, Hedvig, Hedy

Heidi a short form of the German name, Adalheid. See also Adelaide.
Heida, Heidie

Helen (Greek) "light."
Aila, Aileen, Ailene, Aleen, Eileen, Elaine, Elana, Elane, Elayne, Eleanor, Eleanore, Eleen, Elena, Elene, Eleni, Elenore, Eleonora, Eleonore, Elianora, Elinor, Elinore, Ella, Elladine, Elle, Ellen, Ellene, Ellette, Elli, Ellie, Elly, Ellyn, Ellynn, Elna, Elnora, Elora, Elyn, Galina, Helaina, Helena, Hélène, Helenka, Helli, Helyn, Ileana, Ileane, Ilene, Ilona, Ilonka, Jelena, Lana, Leanor, Leena, Lena, Lenka, Lenora, Lenore, Leonora, Leonore, Leora, Lina, Lora, Nell, Nelli, Nellie, Nelly, Nora, Norah, Valenka, Yelena

Helga (Old German) "pious." A form of Olga.

Héloïse a French form of Eloise.

Henrietta (French) "mistress of the household." A feminine form of Henry. See also Harriet.
Enrichetta, Enriqueta, Etta, Etti, Ettie, Etty, Hatti, Hattie, Hatty, Hendrika, Henka, Henrie, Henrieta, Henriette, Henryetta, Hetti, Hettie, Hetty, Yetta, Yettie, Yetty

Hermione (Greek) "of the earth." See also Irma.
Erma, Hermia, Hermina, Hermine, Herminia

Hermosa (Spanish) "beautiful."

Hester (Greek) "star." A Dutch form of Esther.
Hestia, Hettie, Hetty

Hestia (Persion) "a star." Mythological: the goddess of the home.

Hilary (Greek) "cheerful; merry."
Hillary, Hilliary

Hilda (Old German) "woman warrior." A short form of Hildegarde.
Hilde, Hildy

Hildegarde (Old German) "fortress."
Hilda, Hildagard, Hildagarde, Hilde, Hildegaard

Hinda (Hebrew) "hind, female deer."
Hynda

Holly (Old English) "holly tree."
Holli, Hollie

Honey (Old English) "sweet." See also Honora.

Honora (Latin) "honorable."
Honey, Honor, Honoria, Honorine, Nora, Norah, Norri, Norrie, Norry

Hope (Old English) "hope."

Hortense (Latin) "gardener."
Hortensia, Ortensia

Hoshi (Japanese) "star."

Hyacinth (Greek) "hyacinth flower."
Giacinta, Hyacintha, Hyacinthe, Hyacinthia, Hyacinthie, Jacenta, Jacinda, Jacinta, Jacintha, Jacinthe, Jacynth

Ida (Old English) "prosperous"; (Old German) "hardworking."
Idalia, Idalina, Idaline, Idell, Idelle, Idette

Ignacia (Latin) "ardent, fiery." A feminine form of Ignatius.
Ignatia, Ignatzia

Ilana (Hebrew) "big tree."

Ilene a form of Aileen.

Ilka (Slavic) "flattering; industrious." A short form of Ilona.
Ilke, Milka

Ilona (Hungarian) "beautiful." A Hungarian form of Helen.
Ilonka

Ilsa a form of Elsa.

Imena (African) "a dream."

Imogene (Latin) "image."
Emogene, Imogen, Imojean

Ina a Latin feminine suffix added to masculine names. An Irish form of Agnes. See also Inga.
Ina

Inez a Spanish form of Agnes.
Ines, Inesita, Ynes, Ynez

Inga, Inge (Scandinavian) "Inge (an old Germanic hero)." A form of Ingrid.

Ingrid (Scandinavian) "hero's daughter."
Inga, Ingaberg, Ingaborg, Inge, Ingeberg, Ingeborg, Inger, Ingunna

Iola (Greek) "dawn cloud; violet-colored."
Iole

Ione (Greek) "violet-colored stone."
Iona

Iphigenia (Greek) "sacrifice." Mythological: the daughter of the Greek leader Agamemnon. In one myth, she was sacrificed to a goddess; in another, she was saved.
Genia

Irene (Greek) "peace." Mythological: the goddess of peace.
Eirena, Erena, Ira, Irena, Irina, Rena, Rina

Iris (Greek) "rainbow." Mythological: the goddess of the rainbow and messenger of the gods.
Irisa, Irita

Irma (Latin) "noble." See also Hermione.
Erma, Irmina

Isabel (Old Spanish) "consecrated to God." A Spanish form of Elizabeth.
Belia, Belicia, Belita, Bell, Bella, Belle, Ib, Ibbie, Ibby, Isa, Isabeau, Isabelita, Isabella, Isabelle, Iseabal, Isobel, Issi, Issie, Issy, Izabel, Ysabel

Isadora (Latin) "gift of Isis." A feminine form of Isador.
Isidora

Isis (Egyptian) "supreme goddess." Mythological: the moon goddess who rules maternity and fertility.

Isolde (Welsh) "fair lady." Literary: a princess in the Arthurian legends.
Isolda, Isolt, Yseult

Ivory (Latin) "made of Ivory."

Ivy (Old English) "ivy tree."
Ivie

Jacinda (Greek) "beautiful, comely; hyacinth flower." A form of Hyacinth.
Jacenta, Jacey, Jacie, Jacinta, Jacintha, Jacinthe, Jacy, Jacynth

Jackie a short form of Jacoba; Jacqueline.

Jacoba (Hebrew) "supplanter." A feminine form of Jacob.
Jacki, Jackie, Jacky, Jacobina, Jacobine

Jacqueline (Hebrew) "supplanter"; (Old French) "little Jacques." A feminine form of Jacob (through Jacques).
Jackelyn, Jacki, Jackie, Jacklin, Jacklyn, Jackquelin, Jackqueline, Jacky, Jaclin, Jaclyn, Jacquelin, Jacquelyn, Jacquelynn, Jacquenetta, Jacquenette, Jacquetta, Jacquette, Jacqui, Jacquie, Jaquelin, Jaquelyn, Jaquenetta, Jaquenette, Jaquith

Jade (Spanish) "jade."
Jada

Jael (Hebrew) "to ascend."

Jaime (French) "I love." See also Amy; Jaime (m.).

Jamie a feminine form of James.
Jaimie, Jami, Jammie, Jayme, Jaymee

Jamila (Muslim) "beautiful."
Jamilla, Jamille

Jane (Hebrew) "God is gracious." A feminine form of John.
Gene, Gianina, Giovanna, Jaine, Jan, Jana, Janaya, Janaye, Jandy, Janeczka, Janeen, Janel, Janela, Janella, Janelle, Janean, Janene, Janessa, Janet, Janeta, Janetta, Janette, Janey, Jania, Janice, Janie, Janina, Janine, Janis, Janith, Janka, Janna, Jannel, Jannelle, Janot, Jany, Janyte, Jasisa, Jayne, Jaynell, Jean, Jeanette, Jeanie, Jeanne, Jeannette, Jeannine, Jenda, Jenica, Jeniece, Jenni, Jennie, Jenny, Jess, Jessie, Jinny, Jo Ann, Jo-Ann, Joan, Joana, Joanna, Joanne, Joeann, Johanna, Joni, Jonie, Juana, Juanita, Sheena, Shena, Sine, Vania, Vanya, Zaneta

Janet a familiar form of Jane.
Janette, Janot, Jessie

Janice, Janis familiar forms of Jane.

Janna (Arabic) "a harvest of fruit." Also a form of Johanna.
Jana, Janaya, Janaye

Jardena (Hebrew) "to flow downward." A feminine form of Jordan.

Jarietta (Arabic) "earthen water jug."
Jarita

Jasmine (Persian) "jasmine flower."
Jasmin, Jasmina, Jazmin, Jess, Jessamine, Jessamyn, Jessie, Yasmeen

Jay (Medieval Latin) "jaybird."
Jae, Jaycee, Jaye, Jaylene, Jayson

Jean, Jeanne Scottish forms of Jane; Joan.
Gene, Jeana, Jeane, Jeanelle, Jeanette, Jeanie, Jeanine, Jeanna, Jeanne, Jeannette, Jeannie, Jeannine, Jenette, Jennette, Jennica, Jennine

Jeanette a familiar form of Jean.
Jeannette

Jemima (Hebrew) "dove."
Jamima, Jemimah, Jemie, Jemmie, Jemmy

Jena (Arabic) "a small bird."
Jenna

Jennifer (Welsh) "white, fair." A form of Guinevere. See also Genevieve; Gwendolyn.
Genna, Genni, Gennie, Gennifer, Genny, Ginnifer, Jen, Jena, Jeni, Jenifer, Jeniffer, Jenilee, Jenn, Jenna, Jennee, Jenni, Jennica, Jennie, Jennilee, Jenny

Jenny a short form of Jane; Jennifer.

Jerrie, Jerry short forms of Geraldine.
Jeri, Jerrilee, Jerrine, Jerrylee

Jessica (Hebrew) "wealthy." Literary: a name perhaps invented by Shakespeare for a character in *The Merchant of Venice*. A feminine form of Jesse. See also Jasmine.
Jess, Jessalin, Jessalyn, Jesselyn, Jessie, Jessika, Jessy

Jessie a short form of Jasmine; Jessica. A Scottish familiar form of Janet. See also Jesse (m.).
Jessa, Jesse, Jessi

Jewel (Old French) "precious gem."
Jewell, Jewelle

Jezebel (Hebrew) "unexalted, impure." Biblical: the wife of King Ahab.
Jessabell, Jezabel, Jezabella, Jezabelle

Jill a familiar form of Gillian. See also Julia.
Jillana, Jillane, Jillayne, Jilleen, Jillene, Jilli, Jillie, Jilly

Jillian (Latin) "young, downy-haired child." See also Jill; Julia.
Gillian, Jill, Jillana, Jillie, Jilly

Jinny an American familiar form of Virginia. A Scottish familiar form of Jenny.

Jo a short form of Joan; Joanna; Josephine.

Joan (Hebrew) "God is gracious." A form of Jane. A feminine form of John.
Joane, Joanie, Jodi, Jodie, Jody, Joni, Jonie

Joanna, Joanne familiar forms of Jane. Feminine forms of John.
Jo, Joana, Joann, Jo Ann, Jo-Ann, Joeann, Johanna, Johannah

Joby (Hebrew) "persecuted." A feminine form of Job.
Jobey, Jobi, Jobie, Jobina, Jobye, Jobyna

Jocelyn (Latin) "merry"; (Old English) "just." See also Joyce; Justine.
Jocelin, Joceline, Josselyn, Joycelin

Jodi, Jody familiar forms of Joan; Judith.
Jodee, Jodi, Jodie

Joelle (Hebrew) "the Lord is willing." A feminine form of Joel.
Joela, Joell, Joella, Joellen, Joelly, Joelynn

Johnna a feminine form of John; a form of Johanna.
Giana, Gianna, Johna, Johnath, Jonell, Jonis

Jolene (Middle English) "he will increase." A feminine form of Joseph.
Joleen, Joline, Jolyn

Jolie (French) "pretty."
Jolee, Joli, Joly

Jordan (Hebrew) "descending."
Jordain, Jordana, Jordanna, Jorey, Jori, Jorie, Jorrie, Jorry, Jourdan

Josephine (Hebrew) "he shall increase." A feminine form of Joseph.
Fifi, Fifine, Fina, Jo, Joette, Joey, Joline, Josee, Josefa, Josefina, Josepha, Josephina, Josey, Josi, Josie, Josy

Josie a short form of Josephine.
Josee, Josi, Josy

Joy (Latin) "joy." See also Joyce.
Joya, Joyan, Joyann, Joye

Joyce (Latin) "joyous." See also Jocelyn; Joy.
Joice, Joyous

Juanita a Spanish familiar form of Joan.
Juana, Waneta

Judith (Hebrew) "of Judah." Apocryphal: the slayer of Holofernes.
Giuditta, Jodi, Jodie, Jody, Judi, Judie, Juditha, Judy, Judye

Judy a short form of Judith.
Judi, Judie, Judye

Julia (Latin) "youthful." A feminine form of Julius.
Giulia, Giulietta, Joletta, Julee, Juli, Juliana, Juliane, Juliann, Julianne, Julie, Julienne, Juliet, Julieta, Julietta, Juliette, Julina, Juline, Julissa, Julita

Julie a form of Julia.
Juline

June (Latin) "June."
Junette, Junia, Junieta, Junina

Justine (Latin) "just." A feminine form of Justin.
Giustina, Justina, Justinn

Kachine (North American Indian) "sacred dancer."

Kala (Hindi) "black; time."

Kali (Sanskrit) "energy." Mythological: another name for the goddess Shakti, who embodies both creation and destruction.

Kalila (Arabic) "beloved."
Kailey, Kalie, Kalli, Kally, Kaylee, Kaylil, Kylila

Kalinda (Sanskrit) "sun."
Kaleena, Kalina, Kalindi

Kama (Sanskrit) "love." Mythological: the Hindu god of love.

Kamaria (African) "moon-like."

Kameko (Japanese) "child of the tortoise." Mythological: the tortoise symbolizes longevity.

Kamilah (Arabic) "the perfect one."
Kamila, Kamillah

Kanya (Hindu) "virgin."
Kania

Kara a form of Cara; a familiar form of Katherine.
Karalee, Karrah

Karen a Danish form of Katherine.
Caren, Carin, Caron, Caryn, Kari, Karin, Karna, Karon, Karyn, Kerrin

Kari a familiar form of Katherine.
Karee, Karie, Karilynn, Karry, Kary, Karylin

Karla a form of Caroline; Charlotte.

Kate a short form of Katherine.

Katherine (Greek) "pure."
Caitlin, Caitrin, Caren, Carin, Caron, Caryn, Cass, Cassie, Cassy, Catarina, Cate, Caterina, Catha, Catharina, Catharine, Cathe, Cathee, Catherina, Catherine, Cathi, Cathie, Cathleen, Cathlene, Cathrine, Cathryn, Cathy, Cati, Catie, Catlaina, Catriona, Cathyleen, Caty, Caye, Ekaterina, Kakalina, Karen, Karena, Kari, Karin, Karna, Kass, Kassi, Kassia, Kassie, Kata, Katalin, Kate, Katerina, Katerine, Katey, Kath, Katha, Katharine, Katharyn, Kathe, Katheryn, Kathi, Kathie, Kathleen, Kathryn, Kathryne, Kathy, Kathye, Katie, Katina, Katinka, Katrina, Katrine, Katrinka, Katti, Kattie, Katuscha, Katushka, Katya, Kay, Kaye, Ketti, Kettie, Ketty, Kit, Kitti, Kittie, Kitty

Kathleen an Irish form of Katherine.
Kathlin, Katleen, Katlin

Kathy a short form of Katherine, Kathleen, Kathryn.

Katie a short form of Katherine.
Katee, Kati, Katy

Katrina a Greek form of Katherine.
Catrina, Katine

Kay a short form of Katherine.
Caye, Kai, Kaia, Kaja, Kaye

Kayla a form of Kay; Katherine.
Cayla, Kaela, Kaila, Kaylyn

Keely (Irish Gaelic) "beautiful."
Keeley, Keelia

Keiko (Japanese) "adored."

Kelila, Kelula (Hebrew) "crown; laurel."
Kaile, Kayla, Kayle, Kaylee, Kayley, Kyla

Kelly (Irish Gaelic) "warrior woman."
Kelley, Kellen, Kelli, Kellia, Kellie, Kellina

Kelsey (Scandinavian) "from the ship island."
Kelcey, Kelci, Kelcie, Kelcy, Kellsie, Kelsi, Kelsy, Kesley, Keslie

Kendra (Old English) "knowledgeable."
Kendre, Kenna, Kinna

Kerry (Irish Gaelic) "dark; dark-haired."
Keri, Keriann, Kerianne, Kerri, Kerrie

Kesia (African) "favorite."
Kessiah, Kissee, Kissiah, Kissie, Kizzee, Kizzie

Kevyn a feminine form of Kevin.
Kevina

Kiah (African) "season's beginning."
Ki

Kim (Old English) "chief, ruler." A short form of Kimberly.
Kym

Kimberly (Old English) "from the royal fortress meadow."
Cymbre, Kim, Kimberlee, Kimberley, Kimberli, Kimberlyn, Kimbra, Kimmi, Kimmie, Kimmy, Kym

Kiona (North American Indian) "brown hills."

Kip, Kipp (Old English) "from the pointed hill."
Kippie, Kippy

Kira (Persian) "sun." A feminine form of Cyrus.

Kirby (Old English) "from the church town."
Kirbee, Kirbie

Kirima (Eskimo) "a hill."
Kirimia

Kirsten a Scandinavian form of Christine.
Kiersten, Kirsteni, Kirsti, Kirstin, Kristyn, Krystin

Kitty a familiar form of Katherine.

Kora (Greek) "maiden." Mythological: Kore was daughter of Demeter, goddess of agriculture.
Cora, Corabel, Corabella, Corabelle, Corella, Corena, Corene, Coretta, Corette, Corey, Cori, Corie, Corina, Corinna, Corinne, Coriss, Corissa, Corrina, Corrine, Corry, Kore, Korella, Koren, Koressa, Kori, Korie

Kristen a Scandinavian form of Christine.
Krista, Kristan, Kristel, Kristi, Kristin, Kristina, Kristyn, Krysta, Krystyna

Kristin a form of Kristen.

Kristina, Kristine forms of Christina; Christine.

Krystal a form of Crystal.
Kristal, Krystalle, Krystle

Kyle (Irish Gaelic) "handsome; living near the chapel."
Kial, Kiele, Kiley, Kyla, Kylen, Kylie, Kylynn

Kyrene (Greek) "lord, god."
Kyra

Lacey a familiar form of Larissa.
Lacee, Lacie

Ladonna (French) "the lady."

Lainey a familiar form of Elaine.

Lana an English form of Helen. A short form of Alanna. See also Lane; Linette.
Lanae, Lanette, Lanna, Lanny

Lane (Middle English) "from the narrow road."
Laina, Laney, Lanie, Lanni, Lanny, Layne

Lani (Hawaiian) "sky."
Lanita

Lara (Latin) "shining; famous." See also Laraine; Laura; Lorraine.

Laraine (Latin) "sea-bird; gull." A form of Lorraine. See also Lara; Laura.
Larina, Larine

Larissa (Greek) "cheerful."
Lacey, Laryssa, Lissa

Lark (Middle English) "skylark."

Lashonde a form of Melisande.
Lashoh, Lashond, Lashonda, Lashondra

Latona (Greek) Mythological: the powerful deity and mother of Apollo and Diana."
Latonia, Latoya, Latoye, Latoyia

Latrice a diminutive form of Letitia.
Latreece, Latreese, Latreshia, Latricia, Letreece, Letrice

Laura (Latin) "crown of laurel leaves." A feminine form of Lawrence. See also Lara; Laraine; Lorraine.
Lari, Lauralee, Lauré, Laureen, Laurel, Laurella, Lauren, Laurena, Laurene, Lauretta, Laurette, Lauri, Laurice, Laurie, Lora, Loree, Loreen, Loren, Lorena, Lorene, Lorenza, Loretta, Lorette, Lori, Lorinda, Lorita, Lorna, Lorri, Lorrie, Lorry

Lauren an English form of Laura.
Lauryn, Lorne, Lorrin

Lavelle (Latin) "cleansing."
Lavella

Laverne (Old French) "from the grove of alder trees"; (Latin) "springlike."
Laverna, La Verne, Verna

Lavinia (Latin) "purified."
Lavena, Lavina, Lavinie, Vin, Vinni, Vinnie, Vinny

Leah (Hebrew) "weary." Biblical: the wife of Jacob.
Lea, Lee, Leia, Leigh, Leigha, Lia

Leandra (Latin) "like a lioness."
Leandra, Leodora, Leoine, Leoline, Leonanie, Leonelle

Leda (Greek) "lady." A familiar form of Letitia.
Leta, Lida

Lee (Irish Gaelic) "poetic"; (Old English) "from the pasture meadow." A short form of Leah.
Leann, Leanna, Leeann, Leeanne, LeeAnn, Leigh

Leigh (Old English) "from the meadow." A form of Leah; Lee.

Leila (Arabic) "dark as night."
Layla, Leela, Leelah, Leilah, Lela, Lelah, Leland, Lelia, Leyla

Leilani (Hawaiian) "heavenly flower." See also Lani.

Lena (Latin) "temptress." A short form of names ending in "leen," "lena," "lina," and "line."
Lenee, Lenette, Lina

Lenore a Russian form of Eleanor.
Lenora, Leonor

Leona (Latin) "lion." A feminine form of Leo. See also Leontine.
Leoine, Leola, Leone, Leonelle, Léonie

Leonora a form of Eleanor.
Leonore, Nora, Norah

Leontine (Latin) "lionlike." See also Leona.
Leontyne, Léontyne

Leora a familiar form of Eleanor.

Leotie (North American Indian) "prairie flower."

Leslie (Scottish Gaelic) "from the gray fortress."
Lesley, Lesli, Lesly, Lezlie

Letitia (Latin) "joy."
Laetitia, Latashia, Latia, Latisha, Latreshia, Latrice, Leda, Leisha, Leshia, Let, Leta, Lethia, Leticia, Letisha, Letizia, Letta, Letti, Lettie, Letty, Loutitia, Tish, Tisha

Levana (Hebrew) "moon; white."
Levania, Levona

Levina (Latin) "flash, lightning."

Lian (Chinese) "the graceful willow."
Liane, Lianne

Liana (French) "to bind, to wrap around."
Lianna

Libby a familiar form of Elizabeth.
Lib, Libbey, Libbie

Lida (Slavic) "beloved of the people."
Lyda

Lila a short form of Dalila; Delilah; Lillian.

Lilac (Persian) "lilac flower; blue-purple."

Lilith (Arabic) "of the night." Apocryphal: the first wife of Adam. See also Lillian.
Lillis, Lilly, Lily

Lilla (African) "to ascend, to climb."

Lillian (Latin) "lily flower." See also Lilith.
Lil, Lila, Lilas, Lili, Lilia, Lilian, Liliane, Lilias, Lilla, Lilli, Lillie, Lilly, Lily, Lilyan, Liuka

Lily (Latin) "lily flower." A familiar form of Lilith; Lillian.
Lil, Lili, Lilli, Lillie, Lilly

Lina a short form of names ending in "leen," "lena," "lene," "lina," and "line."

Linda (Spanish) "pretty." A short form of names ending in "linda."
Lind, Lindi, Lindie, Lindy, Lynda, Lynde, Lyndy

Lindsay, Lindsey (Old English) "from the linden tree island."
Lind, Lindsy, Linzy, Lyndsay, Lyndsey, Lyndsie, Lynsey

Linette (Celtic) "graceful"; (Old French) "linnet (bird)." See also Lana; Lynn.
Lanette, Linet, Linnet, Lynette, Lynnet, Lynnette

Linnea (Scandinavian) "lime tree."
Linea, Lynea, Lynnea

Lisa a familiar form of Elizabeth. A short form of names ending in "lisa" or "lise."
Leesa, Liesa, Lise, Lisetta, Lisette

Lisha (Arabic) "the darkness before midnight."
Lishe

Liza a familiar form of Elizabeth.
Lizette, Lizzie

Lois a form of Louise.

Lola a familiar form of Dolores; Louise.

Lolita a Spanish familiar form of Lola.
Lita, Lulita

Lomasi (North American Indian) "pretty flower."

Lona (Middle English) "solitary."
Lonee, Loni, Lonna, Lonni, Lonnie

Lora, Lori forms of Laura.
Loree, Loria, Lorianna, Lorianne, Lorie, Lory

Lorelei (German) "alluring." Mythological: the Lorelei were sirens of the river Rhine.
Loralee, Loralie, Loralyn, Lorilee, Lorilyn, Lura, Lurette, Lurleen, Lurlene, Lurline

Lorelle (Latin, Old German) "little."

Loretta a familiar form of Laura.

Lorna Literary: a name probably coined by Richard Blackmore in *Lorna Doone.* A form of Laura.

Lorraine (French) "from Lorraine." See also Lara; Laura.
Laraine, Lorain, Loraine, Lori, Lorine, Lorrayne

Lottie a short form of Charlotte.
Lotta, Lotte, Lotti, Lotty

Lotus (Greek) "lotus flower."

Lou a short form of Louella; Louise.

Louise (Old German) "famous woman warrior." A feminine form of Louis. See also Luella.
Alison, Allison, Aloise, Aloisia, Aloysia, Eloisa, Eloise, Héloïse, Lois, Loise, Lola, Lolita, Lou, Louisa, Louisette, Loyce, Lu, Ludovika, Luisa, Luise, Lulita, Lulu

Love (Old English) "love."

Luana (Old German-Hebrew) "graceful woman warrior."
Lewanna, Louanna, Louanne, Luane, Luann, Luanni, Luwana

Lucille a familiar form of Lucy.
Lucila, Lucilla

Lucinda a familiar form of Lucy.
Cindy, Lucky

Lucretia (Latin) "riches, reward."
Lucrèce

Lucy (Latin) "light; lightbringer." A feminine form of Lucius; Luke.
Lu, Luce, Luci, Lucia, Luciana, Lucie, Lucienne, Lucilla, Lucille, Lucina, Lucinda, Lucine, Lucita, Luz

Ludmilla (Slavic) "loved by the people."
Ludie, Ludovika

Luella (Old English) "elf."
Loella, Lou, Louella, Lu, Luelle, Lula, Lulu

Lulu a familiar form of Louise; Luella.

Luna (Latin) "moon."
Lunetta, Lunette, Lunneta, Lunnete

Lurleen, Lurlene modern forms of Lorelei.
Lura, Lurette, Lurline

Lydia (Greek) "from Lydia." Geographical: Lydia was an ancient land once ruled by Midas.
Lidia, Lydie

Lynette a familiar form of Linette; Lynn.

Lynn (Old English) "waterfall; pool below a fall." A short form of names containing "lin," "line," or "lyn." See also Linette.
Lin, Linell, Linn, Linnell, Lyn, Lyndel, Lyndell, Lynelle, Lynette, Lynna, Lynne, Lynnell, Lynnelle, Lynnett, Lynnette

Mabel (Latin) "lovable."
Amabel, Mab, Mabelle, Mable, Maible, Maybelle

Mackenzie (Irish Gaelic) "son of the wise leader."
Kenzie

Madeline (Greek) "Magdalene, woman from Magdala." See also Maida.
Dalenna, Lena, Lenna, Lina, Linn, Lynn, Lynne, Mada, Madalena, Madalyn, Maddalena, Maddi, Maddie, Maddy, Madel, Madelaine, Madeleine, Madelena, Madelene, Madelina, Madella, Madelle, Madelon, Madge, Madlen, Madlin, Mady, Magda, Magdala, Magdalena, Magdalene, Maidel, Maighdlin, Mala, Malena, Malina, Marleah, Marleen, Marlena, Marlene, Marline, Maud, Maude

Madge a familiar form of Madeline; Margaret.

Mae a form of May.

Maeve a form of Mauve.

Magena (North American Indian) "the coming moon."
Magen

Maggie a familiar form of Margaret.
Maggee

Mahalia (Hebrew) "affection."
Mahala

Maia (Greek) "mother or nurse." Mythological: the daughter of Atlas and Pleione; the goddess of springtime.
Maiah, Maya, Mya

Maida (Old English) "maiden" See also Madeline.
Maddie, Maddy, Mady, Magda, Maidel, Maidie, Mayda

Maisie a familiar form of Margaret.
Maisey

Malka (Hebrew) "queen."
Malkah

Mallory (French) "the mailed" (referring to a knight's armor.
Mallorie, Malorie, Malory

Mamie a familiar form of Margaret.

Manda (Spanish) "battle maiden."
Mandy

Mandy a familiar form of Amanda; Manda; Melinda.

Manuela (Spanish) "God is with us." A feminine form of Emmanuel.

Mara a form of Mary. A short form of Amara; Damara.
Mari

Marcella (Latin) "belonging to Mars; warlike." A feminine form of Mark. See also Marcia.
Marcela, Marcelle, Marcellina, Marcelline, Marchelle, Marcile, Marcille, Marcy, Marquita, Marsiella

Marcia (Latin) "warlike." A feminine form of Mark. See also Marcella.
Marcelia, Marcie, Marcile, Marcille, Marcy, Marquita, Marsha

Marcie, Marcy familiar forms of Marcella; Marcia.
Marci

Margaret (Greek) "pearl."
Greta, Gretal, Gretchen, Gretel, Grethel, Gretta, Madge, Mag, Maggi, Maggie, Maggy, Maiga, Maisie, Marga, Margalo, Margareta, Margarete, Margaretha, Margarethe, Margaretta, Margarette, Margarita, Marge, Margery, Marget, Margette, Margie, Margit, Margo, Margot, Margret, Marguerita, Marguerite, Marquita, Margy, Marji, Marjie, Marjorie, Marjory, Marketa, Meg, Megan, Meggi, Meggie, Meggy, Meghan, Meta, Peg, Pegeen, Peggi, Peggie, Peggy, Rita

Margery a familiar form of Margaret.
Marge, Margi, Margie, Margy, Marje, Marjie, Marjorie, Marjy

Margo, Margot French familiar forms of Margaret.
Margaux, Margeaux

Marguerite a French form of Margaret.

Maria a form of Mary.
Mareah, Mariya

Marian a combination of Mary + Ann. See also Miriam.
Mariam, Mariana, Marianna, Marianne, Marion, Maryann, Maryanne

Maribel a combination of Mary + Belle. See also Mirabel.
Maribelle, Marybelle

Marie a French form of Mary.
Mari

Mariel a Dutch form of Mary.
Mariele, Marielle

Marietta a familiar form of Mary.

Marilla (Hebrew, Old German) "Mary of the fine mind."

Marilyn a familiar form of Mary. See also Marlene; Merry.
Marilee, Marilin, Marylin, Merrili

Marina (Latin) "from the sea." See also Maris.
Marena, Marinna, Marna, Marne, Marni, Marnie

Maris (Latin) "of the sea." A short form of Damara. See also Marina; Mary.
Marisa, Marissa, Marris, Marys, Meris

Marissa a form of Maris.
Maressa, Marisa, Marrissa, Merissa, Morissa

Marjorie a form of Margery.
Marje, Marjie

Marlene a form of Madeline. See also Marilyn.
Marla, Marlane, Marlee, Marleen, Marlena, Marley, Marlyn, Marna

Marlo a form of Mary.

Marnie a familiar form of Marina. See also Marlene.
Marna, Marne, Marney, Marni

Marsha a form of Marcia.

Martha (Aramaic) "lady." Biblical: a sister of Mary.
Marta, Martelle, Marthe, Marthena, Marti, Martie, Martina, Martita, Marty, Martynne, Matti, Mattie, Matty, Pat, Patti, Pattie, Patty

Mary (Hebrew) "bitter." Biblical: the mother of Jesus.
Mair, Maire, Malia, Mame, Mamie, Manon, Manya, Mara, Marabel, Maren, Maria, Mariam, Marian, Marianna, Marianne, Marice, Maridel, Marie, Mariel, Marietta, Marilee, Marilin, Marilyn, Marin, Marion, Mariquilla, Mariska, Marita, Maritsa, Marja, Marje, Marla, Marlo, Marnia, Marya, Maryann, Maryanne, Marylin, Marysa, Masha, Maura, Maure, Maureen, Maurene, Maurine, Maurise, Maurita, Maurizia, Mavra, Meridel, Meriel, Merrili, Mimi, Minette, Minnie, Minny, Miriam, Mitzi, Moira, Mollie, Molly, Muire, Murial, Muriel, Murielle

Maryann a form of Marian.
Mariann, Marianne, Maryanna

Marybeth a combination of Mary + Beth.
Maribeth

Maryellen a combination of Mary + Ellen.
Mariellen

Maryjo a combination of Mary + Joanne.
Marijo

Marylou a combination of Mary + Louise.
Maryl, Meryl

Matilda (Old German) "powerful in battle."
Maitilde, Matelda, Mathilda, Mathilde, Matilde, Matti, Mattie, Matty, Maud, Maude, Tillie, Tilly

Mattie, Matty short forms of Matilda.

Maud, Maude familiar forms of Madeline; Matilda.
Maudie

Maura an Irish form of Mary; Maureen. See also Moira.

Maureen (Old French) "dark-skinned." An Irish familiar form of Mary. A feminine form of Maurice.
Maura, Maurene, Maurine, Maurise, Maurita, Maurizia, Moira, Mora, Moreen, Morena, Moria

Mauve (French) a plant of the purple-colored mallow family.
Maeve

Mavis (French) "thrush." A form of Damara.

Maxine (Latin) "greatest." A feminine form of Max.
Max, Maxi, Maxie, Maxy

May (Latin) "great." Mythological: Maia was goddess of springtime.
Mae, Maia, Maye, Mei

Mead, Meade (Greek) "honey wine."

Meara (Irish Gaelic) "mirth."

Meg a familiar form of Margaret; Megan.

Megan (Greek) "great." An Irish form of Margaret.
Maegan, Meagan, Meaghan, Meg, Megen, Meggi, Meggie, Meggy, Meghan, Meghann

Melanie (Greek) "dark-clothed."
Malanie, Mel, Mela, Melania, Melany, Mella, Melli, Mellie, Melloney, Melly, Melonie, Melony, Milena

Melantha (Greek) "dark flower."

Melba (Greek) "soft; slender"; (Latin) "mallow flower." A feminine form of Melvin.
Malva, Melva

Melina (Latin) "canary-yellow-colored." See also Madeline; Melinda.

Melinda (Greek) "dark, gentle."
Linda, Lindy, Linnie, Lynda, Malina, Malinda, Malinde, Malynda, Mandy, Melinde

Melisande a French familiar form of Melissa; Millicent.
Lisandra, Melisandra

Melissa (Greek) "honey bee."
Lissa, Malissa, Mallissa, Mel, Melesa, Melessa, Melicent, Melisa, Melisande, Melise, Melisenda, Melisent, Melisse, Melita, Melitta, Mellicent, Mellie, Mellisa, Melly, Melosa, Milicent, Milissent, Milli, Millicent, Millie, Millisent, Milly, Misha, Missie, Missy

Melody (Greek) "song."
Melodie

Melvina (Celtic) "like a chieftain." A feminine form of Melvin.
Malvina, Melva, Melvena

Mercedes (Spanish) "mercies." Religious: the name honors *Santa Maria de Mercedes,* "Mary of Mercies." See also Mercy.

Mercy (Middle English) "compassion, mercy."
Merci, Mercie, Mersey

Meredith (Welsh) "guardian from the sea."
Meredithe, Meridith, Merridie, Merry

Meriel a familiar form of Muriel.

Merle (Latin-French) "blackbird."
Merl, Merla, Merlina, Merline, Merola, Meryl, Myrle, Myrlene

Merry (Middle English) "merry." A short form of Meredith. See also Marilyn.
Marrilee, Marylee, Merrie, Merrielle, Merrile, Merrilee, Merrili, Merrily

Mia (Italian) "mine, my." A familiar form of Michelle (from Micaela).

Michael (Hebrew) "who is like the Lord?" See also Michelle.
Micah, Michaela, Michal, Micheal, Mikal, Mycah, Mychael, Mychal

Michelle (Hebrew) "who is like the Lord?" A feminine form of Michael.
Mechelle, Mia, Micaela, Michaela, Michaelina, Michaeline, Michaella, Michal, Michel, Michele, Michelina, Micheline, Michell, Micki, Mickie, Micky, Midge, Miguela, Miguelita, Mikaela, Misha, Miquela

Michiko (Japanese) "the righteous way."
Miche, Michi

Mildred (Old English) "gentle counselor."
Mil, Mildrid, Milli, Millie, Milly

Millicent (Old German) "industrious." A form of Melissa.
Lissa, Mel, Melicent, Melisande, Melisenda, Mellicent, Mellie, Mellisent, Melly, Milicent, Milissent, Milli, Millie, Millisent, Milly, Milzie, Missie, Missy

Millie, Milly short forms of Camille; Emily; Melissa; Mildred; Millicent.

Mimi a French familiar form of Miriam.

Minda (Indian) "knowledge."
Mindy

Mindy a familiar form of Melinda; Minda; Minna.
Mindi

Minerva (Greek) "wisdom." Mythological: the goddess of wisdom.
Minnie, Minny, Myna

Minna (Old German) "tender affection." A short form of Wilhelmina.
Mina, Minetta, Minette, Minne, Minnie, Minny, Minta

Minnie a familiar form of Minerva; Minna; Wilhelmina.

Mira (Latin) "wonderful." A short form of Mirabel; Miranda.
Mireille, Mirella, Mirelle, Mirielle, Mirilla, Myra, Myrilla

Mirabel (Latin) "of extraordinary beauty." See also Miranda.
Mira, Mirabella, Mirabelle

Miranda (Latin) "admirable." Literary: the heroine of Shakespeare's *The Tempest*.
Mira, Miran, Myra, Myranda, Randa

Miriam (Hebrew) "bitter." The original Hebrew form of Mary.
Mimi, Mitzi

Missy a familiar form of Melissa; Millicent.

Misty (Old English) "covered with a mist."
Misti

Mitzi a familiar form of Miriam.

Modesty (Latin) "modest."
Modesta, Modestia, Modestine

Moira (Irish Gaelic) "great." An Irish form of Mary. See also Maura; Maureen.
Moyra

Mollie, Molly Irish familiar forms of Mary.
Mollee, Molli

Mona (Greek) "solitary"; (Irish Gaelic) "noble." A short form of Monica. See also Myrna.
Moina, Monah, Moyna

Monica (Latin) "advisor."
Mona, Monika, Monique

Morgana (Welsh) "edge of the sea." A feminine form of Morgan. Literary: Morgan Le Fay was the sister of King Arthur.
Morgan, Morganica, Morganne, Morgen

Moriah (Hebrew) "God is my teacher."

Moselle (Hebrew) "child rescued from the water." A feminine form of Moses.
Mozelle

Muriel (Arabic) "myrrh"; (Irish Gaelic) "sea-bright." A form of Mary.
Meriel, Murial, Murielle

Myra (Old French) "quiet song." A form of Mira; Miranda.

Myrna (Irish Gaelic) "polite; gentle." See also Mona.
Merna, Mirna, Moina, Morna, Moyna

Myrtle (Greek) "myrtle."
Myrta, Myrtia, Myrtice, Myrtie

Nadia a Slavic form of Nadine.

Nadine (French-Slavic) "hope." A feminine form of Nathan.
Nada, Nadean, Nadeen, Nadia, Nadiya, Nady, Nadya, Natka

Nalani (Hawaiian) "calmness of the heavens."

Nan a familiar form of Ann.
Nana, Nance, Nancee, Nancey, Nanci, Nancie, Nancy, Nanette, Nanice, Nanine, Nannie, Nanny, Nanon, Netti, Nettie, Netty

Nancy a familiar form of Nan.
Nance, Nancee, Nancey, Nanci, Nancie, Nanice, Nannie, Nanny

Nanette a familiar form of Nan.
Netti, Nettie, Netty

Nani (Hawaiian) "beautiful."

Naomi (Hebrew) "pleasant." Biblical: a friend of Ruth.
Naoma, Noami, Noemi, Nomi

Nara (North American Indian, Japanese) "oak."

Nari (Japanese) "thunderpeal."
Nariko

Nasya (Hebrew) "miracle of God."
Nasia

Natalie (Latin) "Christmas, born on Christmas day." See also Noel.
Nat, Nata, Natala, Natalee, Natalina, Nataline, Natalya, Natasha, Nathalia, Nathalie, Natividad, Natty, Netti, Nettie, Netty

Natasha a Russian familiar form of Natalie.
Nastassia

Neala (Celtic) "like a chief." A feminine form of Neal.
Neila, Neile, Neilla, Neille

Neda (Slavic) "born on Sunday." A feminine form of Edward.
Nedda, Nedi

Nelia a short form of Cornelia.
Neely

Nell a familiar form of Cornelia; Eleanor.
Nellie, Nelly

Neona (Greek) "new moon."

Nerine (Greek) "sea nymph."

Nerissa (Greek) "of the sea."
Nerita

Nessie a familiar form of Agnes.

Nettie, Netty familiar forms of Nan; Natalie. Short forms of names ending in "netta," "nette."

Neva (Spanish) "snowy."
Nevada

Niabi (North American Indian) "a fawn."

Nicole (Greek) "victory of the people." A feminine form of Nicholas. See also Nike.
Colette, Cosetta, Cosette, Nichol, Nichole, Nicholle, Nicki, Nickie, Nicky, Nicol, Nicola, Nicolea, Nicolette, Nicoli, Nicolina, Nicoline, Nicolle, Niki, Nikki, Nikoletta, Nikolia

Nike (Greek) "victory." See also Nicole.
Nika

Nikki a familiar form of Nicole.
Niki

Nina (Spanish) "girl." A familiar form of Ann.
Niña, Ninetta, Ninette, Ninnetta, Ninnette, Ninon

Nissa (Scandinavian) "friendly elf or brownie." See also Nyssa.
Nisse, Nissie, Nissy

Nita (North American Indian) "bear." A Spanish familiar form of Ann (from Juanita).

Noel (Latin-French) "Christmas, born on Christmas day." See also Natalie.
Noell, Noella, Noelle, Noellyn, Noelyn, Novelia

Noelani (Hawaiian) "beautiful one from heaven." See also Noel.

Nola (Latin) "small bell." An Irish form of Olivia.
Nolana

Nona (Latin) "the ninth." Mythological: one of the three Fates.
Nonah, Noni, Nonie, Nonna, Nonnah

Nora, Norah short forms of Eleanor; Honora; Leonora.

Noreen an Irish familiar form of Norma.
Norina, Norine

Norma (Latin) "rule, pattern."
Noreen

Novia (Latin) "newcomer"; (Spanish) "sweetheart."
Nova

Nydia (Latin) "from the nest."

Nyssa (Greek) "beginning." See also Nissa.

Octavia (Latin) "eighth; eighth child." A feminine form of Octavius.
Octavie, Ottavia, Tavia, Tavie, Tavy

Odelia (Hebrew) "I will praise God"; (Old Anglo-French) "little and wealthy." A feminine form of Odell.
Odele, Odelinda, Odella, Odelle, Odetta, Odette, Odilia, Odille, Otha, Othelia, Othilia, Ottilie, Uta

Odetta a form of Odelia.

Olethea (Latin) "truth."
Alethea, Oleta

Olga (Scandinavian) "holy."
Elga, Helga, Olenka, Olia, Olive, Olivia, Olva

Oliana (Polynesian) "oleander."

Olivia (Latin) "olive tree." An English form of Olga.
Liv, Liva, Livia, Livvie, Livvy, Nola, Nolana, Nollie, Olga, Olia, Olive, Olivette, Ollie, Olly, Olva

Olympia (Greek) "heavenly."
Olimpia, Olympe, Olympie

Ona a form of Una.
Oona

Ondine (Latin) "wave, wavelet." Mythological: the Undines were water sprites.
Undine

Oneida, Onida (North American Indian) "expected."

Oona an Irish form of Una.

Opal (Hindu) "precious stone."
Opalina, Opaline

Ophelia (Greek) "serpent." Mythological: the serpent signified immortality.
Filia, Ofelia, Ofilia, Ophélie, Phelia

Oralie a French form of Aurelia.

Oriana (Latin) "dawning; golden."
Oriane

Oriole (Latin) "fair-haired."
Oriel

Page (French) "useful assistant."

Paige (Old English) "child; young."

Palila (Polynesian) "bird."

Palma (Latin) "palm tree."
Palmer, Palmira

Paloma (Spanish) "dove."

Pamela (Greek) "all-honey."
Pam, Pamelina, Pamella, Pammi, Pammie, Pammy

Pandora (Greek) "all-gifted."

Pansy (Greek) "fragrant."
Pansie

Patience (French) "enduring expectation."

Patricia (Latin) "of the nobility." A feminine form of Patrick.
Pat, Patrica, Patrice, Patrizia, Patsy, Patti, Patty, Tricia, Trish

Patsy, Patti, Patty short forms of Patricia.

Paula (Latin) "small." A feminine form of Paul.
Paola, Paolina, Paule, Pauletta, Paulette, Pauli, Paulie, Paulina, Pauline, Paulita, Pauly, Pavla, Polly

Paulette a familiar form of Paula.

Pauline a familiar form of Paula.
Paulina

Pazia (Hebrew) "golden."
Paz, Paza, Pazice, Pazit

Peace (Middle English) "the peaceful."

Pearl (Latin) "pearl."
Pearla, Pearle, Pearline, Perl, Perla, Perle, Perry

Peg, Peggy familiar forms of Margaret (from Meg).
Pegeen

Pelagia (Greek) "the sea."
Pelage

Penelope (Greek) "weaver."
Pen, Penelopa, Penny

Penny a short form of Penelope.
Pennie

Pepita (Spanish) "she shall add."
Pepi, Peta

Perry (French) "pear tree"; (Welsh) "son of Harry." A familiar form of Pearl.
Perri

Petra (Greek, Latin) "rock or like a rock." A feminine form of Peter.
Perrine, Pet, Peta, Petrina, Petronella, Petronia, Petronilla, Petronille, Pier, Pierette, Pierrette, Pietra

Petula (Latin) "seeker."
Petulah

Petunia (North American Indian) "petunia flower."

Phedra (Greek) "bright."
Faydra, Phaedra, Phaidra

Philana (Greek) "lover of mankind." A feminine form of Philander.
Phila, Philina, Philine, Phillane

Philippa (Greek) "lover of horses." A feminine form of Philip.
Felipa, Filippa, Phil, Philipa, Philippe, Philippine, Phillie, Philly, Pippa, Pippy

Philomena (Greek) "loving song." Mythological: an Athenian princess who was changed into a nightingale by the gods.
Filomena, Mena

Phoebe (Greek) "shining."
Phebe

Phyllis (Greek) "green bough."
Filide, Philis, Phillis, Phylis, Phyllida, Phyllys

Pia (Italian) "devout."

Pilar (Spanish) "pillar." Religious: one of the appellations of the Virgin Mary.
Pilár

Piper (Old English) "player of the pipe."

Pippa, Pippy familiar forms of Philippa.

Placidia (Latin) "the serene."
Placida

Polly a familiar form of Molly; Paula.

Pollyanna a combination of Polly + Ann.

Pomona (Latin) "fertile; apple." Mythological: the goddess of fruit trees and their products.

Poppy (Latin) "poppy flower."

Portia (Latin) "offering."

Prima (Latin) "first; first child."
Primalia

Priscilla (Latin) "from ancient times."
Pris, Prisca, Priscella, Prissie

Prudence (Latin) "foresight; intelligence."
Pru, Prudi, Prudy, Prue

Prunella (Latin) "brown."
Pru, Prue, Nel, Nella, Nellie

Purity (Middle English) "purity."

Quennie (Old English) "queen."
Quenna

Querida (Spanish) "beloved."

Questa (French) "searcher."

Quinn (Old English) "queen."

Quinta (Latin) "five; fifth child." A feminine form of Quentin.
Quentin, Quinn, Quintana, Quintilla, Quintina

Quintessa (Latin) "essence."
Quintie, Tess, Tessa, Tessie

Rabi (Arabic) "breeze."
Rabiah

Rachel (Hebrew) "ewe." Biblical: the wife of Jacob and mother of Joseph.
Rachael, Rachele, Rachelle, Rae, Rahel, Rakel, Raquel, Raquela, Ray, Raychel, Rayshell, Rey, Rochell, Shell, Shelley, Shellie, Shelly

Radmilla (Slavic) "worker for the people."

Rae (Old English) "doe." A familiar form of Rachel.
Raeann, Ralina, Rayna

Ramona (Spanish) "mighty or wise protectress." A feminine form of Raymond.
Ramonda, Romona, Romonda

Randy a short form of Randall (m.); Randolph (m.).
Randa, Randee, Randene, Randi

Rani (Sanskrit) "queen."
Raine, Rana, Ranique, Ranee, Rania, Ranice, Rayna, Raynell

Ranita (Hebrew) "song."
Ranit, Ranite, Ranitta

Raphaela (Hebrew) "blessed healer." A feminine form of Raphael.
Rafa, Rafaela, Rafaelia

Raquel a Spanish form of Rachel.

Rashida (African) "righteous."
Rashidi

Raven (Old English) "like the raven."

Reba a short form of Rebecca.
Rheba

Rebecca (Hebrew) "bound." Biblical: the wife of Isaac.
Becca, Becka, Becki, Beckie, Becky, Bekki, Reba, Rebecca, Rebeca, Rebecca, Rebecka, Rebeka, Rebekah, Rebekkah, Ree, Reeba, Rheba, Riva, Rivalee, Rivi, Rivkah, Rivy

Regan an English form of Regina.

Regina (Latin) "queen."
Raina, Regan, Reggi, Reggie, Regine, Reina, Reine, Reyna, Rina

Reiko (Japanese) "gratitude; propriety."

Remy (French) "from Rheims."

Rena (Hebrew) "song."
Reena

Renata (Latin) "reborn."
Renae, Renate, Rene, Renée, Renie, Rennie

Rene a short form of Irene; Renée.
Renie

Rene (French "from Renata."
Renae, Rene, Renell, Renelle, Renie

Reta (African) "to shake."
Reeta, Rheta, Rhetta

Rhea (Greek) "earth; that which flows from the earth, as rivers."
Rea

Rhiamon (Welsh) Mythological: a witch.
Rhianon, Rhianna, Rianon, Riannon

Rhoda (Greek) "roses; from Rhodes." A form of Rose.
Rhodie, Rhody, Roda, Rodi, Rodie, Rodina

Rhona a form of Rona.
Roana

Rhonda Geographical: a name of southern Wales, possibly meaning "grand."
Ronda

Riane A feminine form of Ryan.
Ryann

Rica a familiar form of Frederica.
Ricca, Ricki, Rickie, Ricky, Riki, Rikki, Rycca

Ricarda (Old German) "powerful ruler." A feminine form of Richard.
Richarda

Richelle A feminine form of Richard.
Richel, Richela, Richella

Richia A feminine form of Richard.

Ricki, Rickie short forms of Frederica; Rica.

Rihana (Muslim) "sweet basil."
Rhiana, Rhianna, Riana, Rianna

Risa (Latin) "laughter."

Rita a short form of Margaret (from Margherita).
Reeta, Rheta

Riva (French) "shore." A short form of Rebecca (from Rivkah).
Ree, Reeva, Rivalee, Rivi, Rivy

Roanna a form of Rosanne. See also Rowena.
Ranna, Roanne, Ronni, Ronnie, Ronny

Roberta (Old English) "shining with fame." A feminine form of Robert.
Bobbe, Bobbette, Bobbi, Bobbie, Bobby, Bobbye, Bobina, Bobine, Bobinette, Robbi, Robbie, Robby, Robena, Robenia, Robin, Robina, Robinett, Robinette, Robinia, Ruperta

Robin, Robyn (Old English) "robin." Familiar forms of Roberta.
Robbi, Robbie, Robbin, Robby, Robbyn, Robena, Robenia, Robina, Robinet, Robinett, Robinette, Robinia

Rochelle (French) "from the little rock." A form of Rachel.
Roch, Rochell, Rochella, Rochette, Roshelle, Shell, Shelley, Shelly

Roderica (Old German) "famous ruler." A feminine form of Roderick.
Rica

Rolanda (Old German) "fame of the land." A feminine form of Roland.

Roma (Latin) "eternal city."
Romaine, Romelle, Romilda, Romina, Romy

Rona (Scandinavian) "mighty power." A feminine form of Ronald.
Rhona, Ronalda

Ronni, Ronnie, Ronny familiar forms of Roanna; Rowena; Veronica.

Rosabel a combination of Rose + Belle.
Rosabella, Rosabelle

Rosalba (Latin) "white rose."

Rosalie an Irish familiar form of Rose.
Rosaleen, Rosalia, Rozalie, Rozele

Rosalind (Spanish) "beautiful rose."
Ros, Rosalinda, Rosalinde, Rosaline, Rosalyn, Rosalynd, Roselin, Roseline, Roslyn, Roz, Rozalin

Rosalyn a combination of Rose + Lynn. A form of Rosalind.

Rosamond (Old German) "famous guardian."
Ros, Rosamund, Rosmunda, Rosemonde, Roz, Rozamond

Rose (Greek) "rose."
Rasia, Rhoda, Rhodia, Rhody, Rois, Rosa, Rosaleen, Rosalia, Rosalie, Rosella, Roselle, Rosene, Rosetta, Rosette, Rosie, Rosina, Rosita, Rosy, Rozalie, Roze, Rozele, Rozella, Rozina, Zita

Roseanne a combination of Rose + Ann.
Ranna, Roanna, Roanne, Rosanna, Rosanne, Roseann, Rozanna

Roselani (English, Polynesian) "heavenly rose."
Roselane, Roseline

Rosemary (Latin) "rosemary (the herb)."
Rosemaria, Rosemarie

Rowena (Old English) "well-known friend."
Ranna, Rena, Ronni, Ronnie, Ronny, Row, Rowe

Roxanne (Persian) "dawn." Literary: the heroine in Edmund Rostand's *Cyrano de Bergerac*.
Rosana, Roxane, Roxanna, Roxanne, Roxi, Roxie, Roxine, Roxy

Ruby (Old French) "ruby."
Rubetta, Rubi, Rubia, Rubie, Rubina

Ruth (Hebrew) "friend of beauty." Biblical: a friend of Naomi.
Ruthe, Ruthi, Ruthie

Ruthann a combination of Ruth + Ann.
Ruthanne

Sabina (Latin) "Sabine woman; woman from Sheba." See also Sabrina; Sheba.
Brina, Sabine, Savina

Sabra (Hebrew) "thorny cactus; to rest." The name for a native-born Israeli girl. See also Sabrina.

Sabrina (Latin) "from the boundary line." See also Sabina; Sabra.
Brina, Zabrina

Sachi (Japanese) "bliss child; joy."
Sachiko

Sadie a familiar form of Sarah.
Sada, Sadye, Saidee, Sydel, Sydelle

Salena (Latin) "salty."
Salina

Sally a familiar form of Sarah.
Sal, Sallee, Salli, Sallie

Salome (Hebrew) "peace." Biblical: a daughter of Herodias.
Saloma, Salomé, Salomi

Samala (Hebrew) "asked of God."
Samale

Samantha (Aramaic) "listener."
Sam, Sammy

Samara (Hebrew) "ruled by God."
Sam, Samaria, Sammy

Samuela (Hebrew) "name of God." A feminine form of Samuel.
Samella, Samuella

Sandra a short form of Alexandra.
Sandi, Sandy, Sandye, Zandra

Sandy a familiar form of Sandra.
Sandi, Sandie, Sandye

Sapphire (Greek) "sapphire stone; sapphire blue."
Sapphira, Sephira

Sara an English form of Sarah.

Sarah (Hebrew) "princess." Biblical: the wife of Abraham and mother of Isaac.
Sadella, Sadie, Sadye, Saidee, Sal, Salaidh, Sallee, Salli, Sallie, Sally, Sara, Sarena, Sarene, Sarette, Sari, Sarine, Sarita, Sayre, Shara, Sharai, Shari, Sharon, Sharona, Sher, Sheree, Sheri, Sherie, Sherri, Sherrie, Sherry, Sherye, Sorcha, Sydel, Sydelle, Zara, Zarah, Zaria

Saree (Arabic) "most noble."
Sari

Sasha a Russian familiar form of Alexandra.
Sacha, Sascha, Sashenka

Savanna (Spanish) "the barren one."
Savannah

Scarlett (Middle English) "scarlet." Literary: Scarlett O'Hara is the heroine of *Gone with the Wind*.

Season (Latin) "sowing, planting."

Seema (Hebrew) "treasure."
Cyma, Seena, Sima, Simah

Selena (Greek) "moon."
Celene, Celie, Celina, Celinda, Celine, Sela, Selene, Selia, Selie, Selina, Selinda, Seline, Sena

Selima (Hebrew) "peaceful." A feminine form of Solomon.
Selimah

Selma (Scandinavian) "divinely protected." A feminine form of Anselm.
Anselma, Zelma

Senalda (Spanish) "a sign."
Sena

Seraphina (Hebrew) "burning, ardent." Religious: the Seraphim were the highest order of angels.
Serafina, Serafine, Seraphine

Serena (Latin) "calm, serene."
Reena, Rena, Sarina, Serene

Shaina (Hebrew) "beautiful." See also Shannon; Sheena.
Shaine, Shanie, Shayna, Shayne

Shana a familiar form of Shannon.

Shandy (Old English) "rambunctious."
Shandee, Shandeigh, Shandie, Shanta, Shantee

Shani (African) "marvelous."

Shanley (Irish Gaelic) "child of the old hero."
Shanleigh, Shanly

Shannon (Irish Gaelic) "small; wise."
Channa, Shana, Shandy, Shane, Shani, Shanon, Shanna, Shannah, Shannen, Shauna, Shawna

Shari a Hungarian form of Sarah.

Sharon (Hebrew) "Sharon, a plain." A form of Sarah (from Sharai).
Charin, Cherin, Shara, Sharai, Shari, Sharla, Sharona, Sherri, Sherrie, Sherry, Sherye

Shawn a feminine form of John (through Sean).
Sean, Seana, Shaun, Shauna, Shawna, Shawnee, Siana, Sianna

Sheba (Hebrew) "from the Sheba." See also Sabina.
Saba

Shea (Irish Gaelic) "from the fairy fort."
Shae, Shay, Shayla, Shaylah, Shaylyn, Shaylynn

Sheena an Irish form of Jane.

Sheila an Irish form of Cecilia.
Selia, Sheela, Sheelagh, Sheelah, Sheilah, Shela, Shelagh, Shelia, Shelley, Shelli, Shellie, Shelly

Shelby (Old English) "from the ledge estate."
Shel, Shelbi, Shelli, Shellie, Shelly

Shelley (Old English) "from the meadow on the ledge." A familiar form of Rachel; Sheila; Shelby; Shirley.
Shell, Shelli, Shellie, Shelly

Sherry a familiar form of Charlotte; Cher; Sarah; Sher; Shirley.
Sheeree, Sheree, Sheri, Sherie, Sherri, Sherrie, Sherye

Sheryl a familiar form of Shirley.
Sherilyn

Shifra (Hebrew) "beautiful."
Schifra, Shifrah

Shina (Japanese) "good; virtue."
Sheena

Shiri (Hebrew) "my song."
Shira, Shirah

Shirley (Old English) "from the bright meadow."
Sher, Sheree, Sheri, Sherill, Sherline, Sherri, Sherrie, Sherry, Sherye, Sheryl, Shir, Shirl, Shirlee, Shirleen, Shirlene, Shirline

Shoshana (Hebrew) "rose." A Hebrew form of Susan.

Shulamith (Hebrew) "peace."
Sula, Sulamith

Sibley (Old English) "sibling; having one parent in common."
Sybley

Sibyl (Greek) "prophetess." Mythological: the Sibyls were oracles who relayed the messages of the gods.
Cybil, Cybill, Sib, Sibbie, Sibby, Sibeal, Sibel, Sibella, Sibelle, Sibilla, Sibley, Sibylla, Sibylle, Sybil, Sybila, Sybilla, Sybille

Silvia a form of Sylvia.
Silvie

Simone (Hebrew) "one who hears." A feminine form of Simon.
Simmie, Simona, Simonette, Simonne

Skylar, Skyler (Dutch) "sheltering."
Skye, Skyla

Solana (Spanish) "sunshine."
Solenne

Sondra a short form of Alexandra.

Sonia a Slavic and Scandinavian form of Sophie.
Sonja, Sonni, Sonnie, Sonny, Sonya, Sunny

Sonnie, Sonny familiar forms of Sonia.

Sophie (Greek) "wisdom."
Sofia, Sofie, Sonia, Sonja, Sonni, Sonnie, Sonny, Sonya, Sophey, Sophi, Sophia, Sophronia, Sunny

Spring (Old English) "springtime."

Stacy a short form of Anastasia.
Stace, Stacee, Stacey, Staci, Stacia, Stacie

Star (English) "star."
Starla, Starlene, Starlin, Starr

Stella (Latin) "star." A short form of Estelle.

Stephanie (Greek) "crowned." A feminine form of Stephen.
Stefa, Stafani, Stefanie, Steffane, Steffi, Steffie, Stepha, Stephana, Stephani, Stephannie, Stephenie, Stephi, Stephie, Stephine, Stesha, Stevana, Stevena

Storm (Old English) "stormy."
Stormi, Stormie, Stormy

Sue a short form of Susan.

Sukey a familiar form of Susan.
Suki

Sula (Icelandic) "large sea bird."

Summer (Old English) "summer."
Sommer, Sumer

Sunny (English) "bright, cheerful." A familiar form of Sonia.
Sunshine

Susan (Hebrew) "lily." Apocryphal: an accused adultress saved by the wisdom of Daniel.
Siusan, Sosanna, Sue, Sukey, Suki, Susana, Susanetta, Susann, Susanna, Susannah, Susanne, Susette, Susi, Susie, Susy, Suzanna, Suzanne, Suzette, Suzi, Suzie, Suzy, Suzzy, Zsa Zsa

Susanna, Susannah forms of Susan.

Susie, Susy short forms of Susan.

Suzanne a form of Susan.

Sybil a form of Sibyl.

Sydney (Old French) "from the city of St. Denis." See also Sidney (m.).
Sydel, Sydelle

Sylvia (Latin) "from the forest."
Silva, Silvana, Silvia, Silvie, Zilvia

Tabina (Arabic) "Muhammed's follower."

Tabitha (Aramaic) "gazelle."
Tabatha, Tabbi, Tabbie, Tabbitha, Tabby

Tacita (Latin) "to be silent."
Tace, Tacy, Tacye

Taffy (Welsh) "beloved."

Taima (North American Indian) "crash of thunder."

Talia (Greek) "blooming." Mythological: Thalia was the Greek muse of comedy.
Tallia, Tallie, Tally, Talyah, Thalia

Tallulah (North American Indian) "leaping water."
Tallie, Tallou, Tally

Tamara (Hebrew) "palm tree."
Tamar, Tamarah, Tamarra, Tamera, Tamma, Tammi, Tammie, Tammy, Tamra

Tami (Japanese) "people."
Tamiko

Tammy (Hebrew) "perfection." A Scottish name, perhaps a familiar form of Thomasina. A short form of Tamara.
Tammi, Tammie

Tani (Japanese) "valley."

Tansy (Greek) "immortality"; (Latin) "tenacious; persistent."
Tandi, Tandie, Tandy

Tanya (Slavic) meaning unknown. See also Titania.
Tanhya, Tania, Tatiana, Tatiania, Tawnya

Tara (Irish Gaelic) "rocky pinnacle." Mythological: Tara was the home of the ancient Irish kings.
Tarah, Tarra, Tarrah, Terra

Taryn a form of Tara.
Taran, Tareyn, Tarryn, Taryne, Teryn, Terryn

Tasha a familiar form of Natasha or Anastasia)
Tawsha

Tate (Old English) "to be cheerful."
Tatum

Taylor (Middle English) "a tailor."
Tayler

Tempest (Old French) "stormy."

Teresa a form of Theresa.

Terry a short form of Theresa. A feminine form of Terence.
Tera, Teri, Terra, Terri, Terrie, Terrye

Tertia (Latin) "the third."
Terchie

Tess a short form of Tessa. A familiar form of Theresa.
Tessi, Tessie, Tessy

Tessa (Greek) "fourth; fourth child." A familiar form of Theresa.
Tess, Tessi, Tessie, Tessy

Thalassa (Greek) "from the sea."

Thalia (Greek) "joyful; blooming." Mythological: one of the Three Graces.

Thea (Greek) "goddess." A short form of Dorothy; Timothea.

Thelma (Greek) "nursling."

Theodora (Greek) "gift of God." A feminine form of Theodore.
Dora, Fedora, Feodora, Ted, Tedda, Teddi, Teddie, Teddy, Tedi, Tedra, Teodora, Theadora, Theda, Thekla, Theo, Theodosia

Theresa (Greek) "reaper."
Tera, Teresa, Terese, Teresina, Teresita, Teressa, Teri, Terri, Terrie, Terry, Terrye, Terza, Tess, Tessa, Tessi, Tessie, Tessy, Thérèse, Tracey, Tracie, Tracy, Tresa, Tressa, Trescha, Zita

Thomasina (Latin-Greek) "little twin." A feminine form of Thomas.
Tammi, Tammie, Thomasa, Thomasin, Thomasine, Toma, Tomasina, Tomasine, Tommi, Tommie, Tommy

Thora (Scandinavian) "thunder." A feminine form of Thor.
Thordia, Thordis, Tyra

Tia (Greek, Egyptian) "princess." Historical: Princess Tia was the sister of the pharoah, King Ramses.

Tierney (Irish Gaelic) "granchild of the lordly."

Tiffany (Greek) "appearance of God."
Tiff, Tiffani, Tiffanie, Tiffi, Tiffie, Tiffy, Tiphani

Tilda a short form of Matilda.
Tildi, Tildie, Tildy, Tillie, Tilly

Timothea (Greek) "honoring God." A feminine form of Timothy.
Thea, Tim, Timi, Timmi, Timmie, Timmy

Tina a short form of names ending in "tina" or "tine."
Teena, Tiena, Tine

Tirza (Hebrew) "cypress tree."
Tierza, Tirzah

Tita (Latin) "title of honor."

Titania (Greek) "giant." Literary: the queen of the fairies in Shakespeare's *A Midsummer Night's Dream*.
Tania, Tita

Toby (Hebrew) "God is good." A feminine form of Tobias.
Tobe, Tobey, Tobi, Tobye, Tova, Tove, Tybi, Tybie

Tommy a short form of Thomasina.
Tomi, Tommi, Tommie

Toni a familiar form of Antoinette.
Tonia, Tonie, Tony

Tory a short form of Victoria.
Torey, Tori, Torie, Torrie

Tracy (Irish Gaelic) "battler"; (Latin) "courageous." A familiar form of Theresa. See Tracey (m.).
Tracee, Tracey, Traci, Tracie

Tricia, Trisha short forms of Patricia.
Trish

Trilby (Old English) "a soft hat."
Trilbi, Trilbie

Trina a familiar form of Katherine (from Katrina).
Trenna

Trinity (Latin) "triad."
Tini, Trinidad

Trista (Latin) "melancholy." A feminine form of Tristan.

Trixie a familiar form of Beatrice.
Trix, Trixy

Trudy (Old German) "beloved." A short form of Gertrude.
Truda, Trude, Trudey, Trudi, Trudie

Tuesday (Old English) "Tuesday."

Twyla (Middle English) "woven of double thread."
Twila

Tyne (Old English) "river."

Udele (Old English) "prosperous."
Udelle

Ula (Celtic) "sea jewel."
Eula, Ulla

Ulani (Polynesian) "cheerful."
Ulane

Ulrica (Old German) "ruler of all." A feminine form of Ulric.
Rica, Ulrika

Umeko (Japanese) "plum-blossom child." Mythological: the flower symbolizes patience.

Una (Latin) "one, united." An Irish form of Agnes. A familiar form of Winifred.
Ona, Oona

Unity (Middle English) "unity."

Ursula (Latin) "little bear." Orsa, Orsola, Sula, Ulla, Ursa, Ursala, Ursola, Ursulina, Ursuline

Valentina (Latin) "strong; healthy." See also Valerie. Teena, Tina, Val, Vale, Valeda, Valene, Valencia, Valentia, Valentine, Valera, Valida, Valina, Valli, Vallie, Vally

Valerie (Latin) "strong." Val, Valaree, Valaria, Vale, Valeria, Valérie, Valery, Valerye, Valli, Vallie, Vally, Valry

Valora (Latin) "strong, valorous." Valorie

Vanessa Literary: a name invented by Jonathan Swift for Esther Vanhomrigh ("van" from the last name + "essa" for Esther). Nessa, Nessi, Nessie, Nessy, Van, Vania, Vanna, Vanni, Vannie, Vanny

Veda (Sanskrit) "wise." Vedette, Veleda, Velda, Vida

Velma a familiar form of Wilhelmina. Vilma

Velvet (Middle English) "velvety."

Venus (Latin) "Venus (goddess of beauty)." Venita, Vin, Vinita, Vinnie, Vinny

Vera (Latin) "true"; (Slavic) "faith." A short form of Veronica. Veradis, Vere, Verena, Verene, Verina, Verine, Verla

Verda (Latin) "young, fresh." Verdi, Verdie

Verena (Old German) "defender." A familiar form of Vera; Verna.

Verna (Latin) "springlike." See also Vera. Vernice

Veronica (Latin-Greek) "true image." A form of Bernice. See also Verena; Verna. Ranna, Ronica, Ronna, Ronni, Ronnica, Ronnie, Ronny, Vera, Veronika, Veronike, Véronique, Vonni, Vonnie, Vonny

Vicki, Vicky short forms of Victoria.

Victoria (Latin) "victory." A feminine form of Victor. Vicki, Vickie, Vicky, Vikki, Vikky, Vitoria, Vittoria

Vida a short form of Davita. Veda, Vita, Vitia

Viola a form of Violet.

Violet (Latin) "violet flower." Eolande, Iolande, Iolanthe, Vi, Viola, Violante, Viole, Violetta, Violette, Yolanda, Yolande, Yolane, Yolanthe

Virginia (Latin) "virginal, maidenly." Ginelle, Ginger, Ginni, Ginnie, Ginny, Jinny, Virgie, Virginie

Vivian (Latin) "full of life." **Vevay, Vi, Viv, Vivi, Vivia, Viviana, Vivianne, Vivie, Vivien, Vivienne, Vivyan, Vivyanne**

Walker (Old English) "thickener of cloth."

Wallis (Old English) "from Wales." A feminine form of Wallace. **Wallie, Wally**

Wanda (Old German) "wanderer." See also Gwendolyn. **Vanda, Wandie, Wandis, Wenda, Wendeline, Wendi, Wendie, Wendy, Wendye**

Wendy a familiar form of Gwendolyn; Wanda. **Wendeline, Wendi, Wendie, Wendye, Windy**

Wesley (Old English) "from the western meadow."

Whitney (Old English) "from the white island; from fair water."

Wilda (Old English) "willow."

Wilhelmina (Old German) "determined guardian." A feminine form of William. **Billi, Billie, Billy, Guglielma, Guillema, Guillemette, Min, Mina, Minna, Minni, Minnie, Minny, Valma, Velma, Vilhelmina, Vilma, Wileen, Wilhelmine, Willa, Willabella, Willamina, Willetta, Willette, Willi, Willie, Willy, Wilma, Wilmette, Wylma**

Willa a short form of Wilhelmina. A feminine form of William. **Willi, Willie, Willy**

Willow (Middle English) "freedom; willow tree."

Wilma a short form of Wilhelmina. **Valma, Vilma**

Wilona (Old English) "desired." **Wilone**

Winna (African) "friend." **Winnah**

Winnie a short form of Gwyneth; Winona; Wynne. **Winni, Winny**

Winnifred (Old German) "peaceful friend." A form of Guinevere. **Freddi, Freddie, Freddy, Fredi, Ona, Oona, Una, Winifred, Winnie, Winne, Winny, Wynn**

Winona (North American Indian) "first-born daughter." **Wenona, Wenonah, Winnie, Winny, Winonah**

Winter (Old English) "winter."

Wren (Old English) "wren."

Wynne (Welsh) "fair." A short form of Gwendolyn; Gwyneth. **Winne, Winnie, Winny, Wynn**

Xanthe (Greek) "golden yellow." **Xantha**

Xaviera (Arabic) "brilliant"; (Spanish Basque) "owner of the new house." A feminine form of Xavier.

Xenia (Greek) "hospitable."
Xena, Zena, Zenia

Xylia (Greek) "of the wood." See also Sylvia.
Xylina

Yasu (Japanese) "the tranquil."

Yesima (Hebrew) "right hand; strength."

Yetta (Old English) "to give; giver." A short form of Henrietta.

Yoko (Japanese) "the positive (female)."

Yolanda (Greek) "violet flower." A French form of Violet (from Violante).
Eolande, Iolande, Iolanthe, Yolande, Yolane, Yolanthe

Yonina (Hebrew) "dove."
Jona, Jonati, Jonina, Yona, Yonah, Yonit, Yonita

Yoshiko (Japanese) "good."
Yoshi

Yvette a familiar form of Yvonne.
Ivett, Ivette, Yevette

Yvonne (Old French) "archer." A feminine form of Ivar; Ives. See also Eve.
Evonne, Ivonne, Yevette, Yvette

Zahara (African) "flower."

Zara (Hebrew) "dawn." A form of Sarah. See also Zerlina.
Zarah, Zaria

Zelda a short form of Griselda.
Selda, Zelde

Zena a form of Xenia.
Zenia

Zenobia (Greek) "sign, symbol."
Zeba, Zeeba, Zeena, Zena

Zetta (Hebrew) "olive."
Zeta, Zetana

Zia (Latin) "kind of grain."
Zea

Zina (African) "name."

Zita a short form of names ending in "sita" or "zita."
Zitella

Zoe (Greek) "life."
Zoë

Zola (Italian) "ball of earth."

Zora (Slavic) "aurora, dawn." See also Zara.
Zorah, Zorana, Zorina, Zorine

Zsa Zsa a Hungarian familiar form of Susan.

Aaron (Hebrew) "enlightened." Biblical: the brother of Moses and first high priest of the Jews.
Aharon, Ari, Arin, Arnie, Arny, Aron, Arron, Erin, Haroun, Ron, Ronnie, Ronny

Abbey a short form of Abbott; Abelard; Abner.
Abbie, Abby

Abbott (Hebrew) "father; abbot."
Ab, Abba, Abbé, Abbey, Abbie, Abbot, Abby, Abott

Abdul (Arabic) "son of." The name may be used with another name or independently.
Ab, Abdel, Del

Abe a short form of Abel; Abelard; Abraham; Abram.
Abey, Abie

Abel (Hebrew) "breath." A short form of Abelard.
Abe, Abey, Abie

Abelard (Old German) "noble and resolute."
Ab, Abbey, Abby, Abe, Abel

Abner (Hebrew) "father of light." Biblical: the commander of King Saul's army.
Ab, Abbey, Abbie, Abby, Avner, Eb, Ebbie, Ebby, Ebner

Abraham (Hebrew) "father of the multitude." Biblical: the first Hebrew patriarch.
Abe, Abey, Abie, Abrahán, Abram, Abramo, Abran, Avram, Avrom, Bram, Ibrahim

Abram (Hebrew) "the lofty one is father." A form of Abraham.
Abe, Abey, Abie, Abramo, Avram, Avrom, Bram

Absalom (Hebrew) "father of peace." Biblical: son of King David.

Ace (Latin) "unity."
Acey, Acie

Ackerley (Old English) "from the meadow of oak trees."
Ackley

Adair (Scottish Gaelic) "from the oak tree ford."

Adam (Hebrew) "man of the red earth." Biblical: the first man created by God.
Ad, Adamo, Adams, Adán, Adão, Addie, Addy, Ade, Adhamh

Adamson (Hebrew) "son of Adam."
Adams

Addison (Old English) "son of Adam."
Ad, Addie, Addy

Adlai (Hebrew) "my witness."
Ad, Addie, Addy

Adler (Old German) "eagle."
Ad

Adolph (Old German) "noble wolf; noble hero."
Ad, Adolf, Adolphe, Adolpho, Adolphus, Dolf, Dolph

Adrian (Latin) "dark."
Ade, Adriano, Adrien, Hadrian

Adriel (Hebrew) "of God's majesty."
Adrial

Ahearn (Celtic) "Lord of the horses."
Ahern

Ahmed (Arabic) "most highly praised."
Ahmad

Aidan (Irish Gaelic) "warmth of the home."
Aiden

Al a short form of names beginning with "al."

Alan (Irish Gaelic) "handsome; cheerful."
Ailin, Al, Alain, Alair, Aland, Alano, Alanson, Allan, Allayne, Allen, Alley, Alleyn, Allie, Allyn, Alon

Alaric (Old German) "ruler of all."
Alric, Alrick, Ulrich

Alastair a Scottish form of Alexander.
Al, Alasdair, Alasteir, Alaster, Alistair, Alister, Allister, Allistir

Alben (Latin) "fair, blond." See also Albert; Alvin.
Al, Alban, Albie, Albin, Alby

Albert (Old English) "noble and bright." See also Alben.
Adelbert, Ailbert, Al, Alberto, Albie, Albrecht, Aubert, Bert, Bertie, Berty, Elbert

Alcott (Old English) "from the old cottage."
Alcot

Alden (Old English) "old, wise protector."
Al, Aldin, Aldwin, Elden, Eldin

Aldous (Old German) "old and wise."
Al, Aldis, Aldo, Aldus

Aldrich (Old English) "old, wise ruler."
Al, Aldric, Aldridge, Alric, Eldridge, Rich, Richie, Richy

Alec, Alex short forms of Alexander.

Alexander (Greek) "helper of mankind." Historical: the name honors Alexander the Great.
Al, Alasdair, Alastair, Alaster, Alec, Alejandro, Alejo, Alek, Aleksandr, Alessandro, Alex, Alexandr, Alexandre, Alexandro, Alexandros, Alexio, Alexis, Alic, Alick, Alisander, Alistair, Alister, Alix, Allister, Allistir, Sander, Sandro, Sandy, Sascha, Sasha, Saunder

Alexis a familiar form of Alexander.
Alexi

Alfonso an Italian form of Alphonse.

Alfred (Old English) "elf counselor; wise counselor."
Al, Alf, Alfie, Alfredo, Alfy, Avery, Fred, Freddie, Freddy

Alger (Old German) "noble spearman." A short form of Algernon.
Al, Algar, Elgar

Algernon (Old French) "bearded."
Al, Alger, Algie, Algy

Ali (Arabic) "greatest."

Allan, Allen forms of Alan.

Allard (Old English) "noble and brave."
Al, Alard

Alonzo a form of Alphonse.
Alonso

Aloysius (Old German) "famous in war."

Alphonse (Old German) "noble and eager."
Al, Alf, Alfie, Alfons, Alfonso, Alfonzo, Alford, Alfy, Alonso, Alonzo, Alphonso, Fons, Fonsie, Fonz, Fonzie

Alton (Old English) "from the old town."
Alten

Alvin (Old German) "beloved by all." See also Alben.
Al, Aloin, Aluin, Aluino, Alva, Alvan, Alvie, Alvy, Alwin, Alwyn, Elvin

Amadeo (Spanish) "beloved of God."
Amadis, Amado, Amando

Ambrose (Greek) "immortal."
Ambie, Ambros, Ambrosi, Ambrosio, Ambrosius, Amby, Brose

Amiel (Hebrew) "lord of my people."

Amory a form of Emery.
Amery

Amos (Hebrew) "burden." Biblical: a Hebrew prophet.

Anastasius (Greek) "one who shall rise again."
Anastas, Anastase, Anastasio, Anastatius, Anastice

Anatole (Greek) "man from the east."
Anatol, Anatolio

Anders a Swedish form of Andrew.
Anderson

André a French form of Andrew.
Andras, Andris

Andrew (Greek) "strong; manly." Biblical: one of the Twelve Apostles.
Anders, Andie, Andonis, Andre, Andrea, Andreas, Andrej, Andres, Andrés, Andrey, Andy, Drew, Dru, Drud, Drugi

Andy a short form of Andrew.
Andie

Angelo (Greek) "angel."
Ange, Angel, Angell, Angie, Angy

Angus (Scottish Gaelic) "unique choice; one strength." Mythological: Angus Og is a Celtic god or spirit of laughter, love, and wisdom.
Ennis, Gus

Ansel (Old French) "adherent of a nobleman."
Ancell, Ansell

Anselm (Old German) "divine warrior."
Anse, Ansel, Anselme, Anselmi, Anselmo, Elmo

Anson (Old German) "of divine origin."
Hanson

Anthony (Latin) "priceless."
Antin, Antoine, Anton, Antone, Antoni, Antonin, Antonino, Antonio, Antonius, Antons, Antony, Tony

Antoine a French form of Anthony.

Antonio an Italian form of Anthony.

Apollo (Greek) "manly." Mythological: the god of prophecy, healing, and the sun.

Archer (Old English) "bowman." A short form of Archibald. See also Ivar; Ives.

Archibald (Old German) "genuinely bold."
Arch, Archaimbaud, Archambault, Archer, Archibaldo, Archibold, Archie, Archy

Archie a familiar form of Archer; Archibald.
Archy

Arden (Latin) "ardent, fiery."
Ard, Ardie, Ardin, Ardy

Aric (Old German) "ruler." Early German form of Richard.
Arick

Ariel (Hebrew) "lion of God."
Airel, Arel, Arie

Aristotle (Greek) "the best."
Ari, Arie, Arri

Arlen (Irish Gaelic) "pledge."
Arlan, Arlin

Arlo (Spanish) "the barberry."

Armand (Old German) "army man." A French form of Herman.
Arman, Armando, Armin

Armstrong (Old English) "strong arm."

Arne (Old German) "eagle." See also Arnold.
Arney, Arni, Arnie

Arnie a short form of Arne; Arnold.

Arnold (Old German) "strong as an eagle; eagle-ruler." See also Arne.
Arnaldo, Arnaud, Arney, Arni, Arnie, Arnoldo, Arny

Arrio (Spanish) "warlike."
Ario

Art, Artie short forms of Artemus; Arthur.

Artemus (Greek) "gift of Artemis; safe and sound."
Artemas, Artemis, Artie, Arty

Arthur (Celtic) "noble"; (Welsh) "bear-hero."
Art, Artair, Arte, Arther, Artie, Artur, Arturo, Artus, Arty, Aurthur

Arvad (Hebrew) "wanderer."
Arv, Arvid, Arvie

Arvin (Old German) "friend of the people; friend of the army." See also Irving.
Arv, Arvie, Arvy

Asa (Hebrew) "physician."
Ase

Ashby (Scandinavian) "from the ash-tree farm."
Ash, Ashbey, Ashton

Asher (Hebrew) "happy; blessed."
Ash

Ashford (Old English) "from the ash-tree ford."
Ash

Ashley (Old English) "from the ash tree meadow."
Ash, Ashlin

Aubrey (Old French) "blond ruler; elf ruler."
Alberik, Aube, Auberon, Avery, Oberon

Audun (Scandinavian) "deserted or desolate."

August (Latin) "majestic dignity." Historical: the name honors Augustus Caesar. See also Augustine.
Agosto, Aguistin, Agustin, Augie, Auguste, Augustin, Augusto, Augustus, Augy, Austen, Austin, Gus, Guss

Augustine (Latin) "belonging to Augustus." Historical: the name honors St. Augustine. See also August.
Aguistin, Agustin, Augie, Augustin, Augy, Austen, Austin, Gus

Aurelius (Latin) "golden."
Aurelio

Austin a form of August; Augustine.
Austen

Averill (Middle English) "April; born in April." See also Avery.
Ave, Averell, Averil

Avery an English form of Alfred; Aubrey. See also Averill.

Avram a Hebrew form of Abraham; Abram.

Axel (Old German) "father of peace." A Scandinavian form of the Hebrew name Absalom.
Aksel, Ax, Axe

Bailey (Old French) "bailiff; steward."
Bail, Bailie, Baillie, Baily

Bainbridge (Irish Gaelic) "fair bridge."
Bain

Baird (Irish Gaelic) "ballad singer."
Bar, Bard, Barde, Barr

Baldwin (Old German) "bold friend."
Bald, Balduin, Baudoin

Balfour (Scottish Gaelic) "pasture land."

Bancroft (Old English) "from the bean field."
Ban, Bank, Banky, Bink, Binky

Barclay (Old English) "from the birch tree meadow." See also Burke.
Bar, Berk, Berkeley, Berkie, Berkley, Berky

Bard an Irish form of Baird.
Bar, Barr

Barnabas (Greek) "son of prophecy." Biblical: a close associate of Paul.
Barnaba, Barnabe, Barnaby, Barnebas, Barney, Barnie, Barny, Burnaby

Barnaby an English form of Barnabas.

Barnett (Old English) "nobleman."
Barn, Barney, Barron, Barry

Barney a familiar form of Barnabas; Barnett; Bernard.

Baron (Old English) "nobleman, baron."

Barret (Old German) "mighty as a bear."
Bar, Barrett, Bear

Barry (Irish Gaelic) "spearlike, pointed"; (Welsh) "son of Harry." A familiar form of Barnett; Baruch; Bernard.
Barri, Barrie, Barris, Bary

Bart a short form of Bartholomew; Barton; Bertram.

Bartholomew (Hebrew) "son of a farmer." Biblical: one of the Twelve Apostles.
Bart, Bartel, Barth, Barthel, Barthélemy, Bartholomeo, Bartholomeus, Bartlet, Bartlett, Bartolomé, Bartolomeo, Bat

Barton (Old English) "from the barley farm."
Bart, Bartie, Barty

Bartram a form of Bertram.

Baruch (Hebrew) "blessed."
Barry

Basil (Latin) "magnificent, kingly."
Base, Basile, Basilio, Basilius, Vasilis, Vassily

Basir (Turkish) "intelligent and discerning."

Baxter (Old English) "baker."
Bax, Baxie, Baxy

Bayard (Old English) "having red-brown hair."
Bay

Beau (Old French) "handsome." A short form of Beauregard.
Beal, Beale, Bealle, Beaufort, Bo

Beauregard (Old French) "beautiful in expression."
Beau, Bo

Beck (Scandinavian) "brook."

Bellamy (Old French) "beautiful friend."
Belamy, Bell

Ben (Hebrew) "son." A short form of names beginning with "ben."
Benn, Bennie, Benny

Benedict (Latin) "blessed."
Ben, Bendick, Bendict, Bendix, Benedetto, Benedick, Benedicto, Benedikt, Bengt, Benito, Bennie, Benny, Benoit

Benjamin (Hebrew) "son of the right hand."
Ben, Beniamino, Benjamen, Benji, Benjie, Benjy, Benn, Bennie, Benny, Benyamin, Jamie, Jim

Benson (Hebrew-English) "son of Benjamin."
Ben, Benn, Bennie, Benny

Bentley (Old English) "from the moor."
Ben, Benn, Bennie, Benny, Bent, Bentlee

Benton (Old English) "of the moors."
Ben, Benn, Bennie, Benny, Bent

Bergren (Scandinavian) "mountain stream."
Berg

Berkeley a form of Barclay.
Berk, Berkie, Berkley, Berkly, Berky

Bern (Old German) "bear." A short form of Bernard.
Berne, Bernie, Berny, Bjorn

Bernard (Old German) "brave bear."
Barnard, Barney, Barnie, Barny, Bear, Bearnard, Bern, Bernardo, Bernarr, Berne, Bernhard, Bernie, Berny, Burnard

Bert (Old English) "bright." A short form of names containing "bert." See also Burton.
Bertie, Berty, Burt, Burty, Butch

Berthold (Old German) "brilliant ruler."
Bert, Berthoud, Bertie, Bertold, Bertolde, Berty

Bertram (Old English) "glorious raven."
Bart, Bartram, Beltrán, Bert, Bertie, Berton, Bertrand, Bertrando, Berty

Bevan (Irish Gaelic) "son of Evan."
Bev, Bevin, Bevon

Bill, Billy familiar forms of William.
Bil, Billie

Bing (Old German) "kettle-shaped hollow."

Birch (Old English) "birch tree."
Birk, Burch

Bishop (Old English) "bishop."
Bish

Bjorn a Scandinavian form of Bern.

Blaine (Irish Gaelic) "thin, lean."
Blane, Blayne

Blair (Irish Gaelic) "from the plain."

Blaise a French form of Blaze.

Blake (Old English) "fair-haired and fair-complected."

Blaze (Latin) "stammerer."
Biagio, Blaise, Blas, Blase, Blasien, Blasius, Blayze

Bo an American form of Beau. A short form of Beauregard; Bogart.

Bob, Bobby familiar forms of Robert.
Bobbie

Bogart (Old French) "strong as a bow."
Bo, Bogey, Bogie

Bond (Old English) "tiller of the soil."
Bondie, Bondon, Bondy

Boone (Old French) "good."
Bone, Boonie, Boony

Booth (Old English) "from the hut."
Boot, Boote, Boothe

Borden (Old English) "from the valley of the boar."
Bord, Bordie, Bordy

Borg (Scandinavian) "from the castle."

Boris (Slavic) "battler, warrior."

Bowie (Irish Gaelic) "yellow-haired."
Bow, Bowen, Boyd

Boyce (Old French) "from the woodland."
Boy, Boycey, Boycie

Boyd an Irish form of Bowie.

Brad (Old English) "broad." A short form of names beginning with "brad."

Braden (Old English) "from the wide valley."
Bradan, Brade

Bradford (Old English) "from the broad river crossing."
Brad, Ford

Bradley (Old English) "from the broad meadow."
Brad, Bradly, Bradney, Lee, Leigh

Bradshaw (Old English) "large virginal forest."

Brady (Irish Gaelic) "spirited"; (Old English) "from the broad island."

Bram (Irish Gaelic) "raven"; (Old English) "fierce; famous." A short form of Abraham; Abram. See also Brand.
Bran

Bramwell (Old English) "of Abraham's well."
Bram

Branch (Latin) "a paw, a claw, or a branch of a tree."

Brand (Old English) "fire-brand." A short form of Brandon.
Bran, Brander, Brandt, Brandy, Brant, Brantley

Brandon (Old English) "from the beacon hill." See also Brendan; Brenton.
Bran, Brand, Branden, Brandy, Brandyn, Brannon

Brendan (Irish Gaelic) "little raven." See also Brandon; Brenton.
Bren, Brenden, Brendin, Brendis, Brendon, Brennan, Brennen, Bryn

Brent (Old English) "steep hill." A short form of Brenton

Brenton (Old English) "from the steep hill." See also Brandon; Brendan.
Brent

Bret, Brett (Celtic) "Briton."
Brit, Britt

Brewster (Old English) "brewer."
Brew, Brewer, Bruce

Brian (Irish Gaelic) "strength; virtue." Historical: Brian Boru was the most famous Irish king.
Briano, Briant, Brien, Brion, Bryan, Bryant, Bryon

Brice a form of Price.
Bryce

Brigham (Old English) "from the enclosed bridge."
Brig, Brigg, Briggs

Brock (Old English) "badger."
Brockie, Brocky, Brok

Broderick (Old English) "from the broad ridge."
Brod, Broddie, Broddy, Broderic, Rick, Rickie, Ricky

Brody (Irish Gaelic) "ditch."
Brodie

Bronson (Old English) "son of the dark-skinned one."
Bron, Bronnie, Bronny, Son, Sonny

Brook (Old English) "from the brook."
Brooke, Brooks

Bruce (Old French) "from the brushwood thicket." See also Brewster.
Brucie, Bruis

Bruno (Italian) "brown-haired."

Bryan, Bryant forms of Brian.

Bryce a form of Brice.

Buck (Old English) "buck deer."
Buckie, Bucky

Bud (Old English) "herald; messenger."
Budd, Buddie, Buddy

Burgess (Old English) "citizen of a fortified town."
Burg, Burr

Burke (Old French) "from the fortress." See also Barclay.
Berk, Berke, Bourke, Burk

Burl (Old English) "cup-bearer"; or from the surname Burrell, "home-spun."
Burlie, Byrle

Burleigh (Old English) "a field with knotted tree trunks."
Burley

Burne (Old English) "from the brook."
Bourn, Bourne, Burn, Byrne

Burris (Old English) "of the town."
Burr

Burt a form of Bert. A short form of Burton.

Burton (Old English) "from the fortress."
Burt

Butch a familiar form of Bert; Burt.

Byrd (Old English) "birdlike."
Byrdie

Byron (Old French) "from the cottage."
Biron, Buiron, Byram, Byran, Byrann, Byrom

Cadell (Celtic) "of material spirit."
Cade, Cadel, Cedell

Caesar (Latin) "long-haired; emperor (through usage as a title for Roman emperors)."
Casar, César, Cesare, Cesaro, Kaiser

Cal a short form of names beginning with "cal."

Calder (Old English) "stream."
Cal

Caldwell (Old English) "dweller by the cold spring."
Cal

Caleb (Hebrew) "bold one; dog."
Cal, Cale, Kaleb

Calhoun (Celtic) "warrior."

Calvert (Old English) "herdsman."
Cal, Calbert

Calvin (Latin) "bald." Historical: John Calvin was a Protestant reformer.
Cal, Calv, Kalvin, Vin, Vinnie, Vinny

Camden (Scottish Gaelic) "from the winding valley."

Cameron (Scottish Gaelic) "crooked nose."
Cam, Camey, Cammy

Campbell (Scottish Gaelic) "crooked mouth."
Cam, Camp, Campy

Canute (Scandinavian) "knot."
Cnut, Knut, Knute

Carey (Welsh) "from near the castle."
Care, Cary

Carl (Old German) "farmer." A Swedish form of Charles. A short form of names beginning with "carl."

Carleton (Old English) "farmer's town."
Carl, Carlton, Charlton

Carlin (Irish Gaelic) "little champion."
Carl, Carlie, Carling, Carly

Carlisle (Old English) "from the fortified town."
Carl, Carlie, Carly, Carlyle

Carlos a Spanish form of Charles.
Carlo

Carmine (Latin) "song."

Carney (Irish Gaelic) "victorious."
Car, Carny, Karney, Kearney

Carr (Scandinavian) "from the marsh."
Karr, Kerr

Carroll (Irish Gaelic) "champion." A familiar form of Charles.
Carolus, Carrol, Cary, Caryl

Carson (Old English) "son of the family on the marsh."

Carter (Old English) "cart driver."
Cart

Carver (Old English) "woodcarver."

Cary a short form of Carey; Carroll.

Casey (Irish Gaelic) "brave."
Case

Casimir (Slavic) "proclamation of peace."
Cas, Casimire, Kazimir

Casper (Persian) "treasurer."
Caspar, Cass, Cassie, Cassy, Gaspar, Gaspard, Gasparo, Gasper, Jasper, Kaspar, Kasper

Cassidy (Irish Gaelic) "clever."
Cass, Cassie, Cassy

Cassius (Latin) "vain."
Cash, Cass, Cassie, Cassy, Caz, Cazzie

Cecil (Latin) "blind."
Cece, Cécile, Cecilio, Cecilius, Celio

Cedric (Old English) "battle chieftain."
Cad, Caddaric, Ced, Rick, Rickie, Ricky

Chad (Old English) "warlike." A short form of names like Chadwick; Chadbourne. A familiar form of Charles.
Chadd, Chaddie, Chaddy

Chadwick (Old English) "from the warrior's town."
Chad, Chadd

Chaim (Hebrew) "life."
Hayyim, Hy, Hyman, Hymie, Mannie, Manny

Chalmers (Scottish Gaelic) "son of the lord."

Chandler (Old French) "candlemaker."
Chan, Chane

Chaney (French) "oak wood." See also Chandler, Channing.
Cheney

Channing (Old English) "knowing"; (Old French) "canon." See also Conan.
Chan, Chane

Chapman (Old English) "merchant."
Chap, Chappie, Chappy, Mannie, Manny

Charles (Old German) "manly; strong." See also Carleton.
Carl, Carlo, Carlos, Carrol, Carroll, Cary, Caryl, Chad, Chaddie, Chaddy, Charley, Charlie, Charlot, Charlton, Chas, Chic, Chick, Chicky, Chip, Chuck, Karel, Karl, Karoly

Charlton a form of Carleton.

Chase (Old French) "hunter."

Chauncey (Middle English) "chancellor; church official."
Chan, Chance, Chancey, Chaunce

Chen (Chinese) "great."

Chester (Old English) "from the fortified camp." A short form of Rochester.
Ches, Cheston, Chet

Chet a short form of Chester.

Chevalier (French) "knight."
Chev, Chevy

Chic, Chick familiar forms of Charles.
Chickie, Chicky

Chico a Spanish familiar form of Francis (from Francisco).

Chilton (Old English) "from the farm by the spring."
Chil, Chill, Chilt

Chris a short form of Christian; Christopher.
Chrisse, Chrissie, Chrissy

Christian (Greek) "follower of Christ."
Chrétien, Chris, Chrissie, Chrissy, Christiano, Christie, Christy, Cristian, Kit, Kris, Krispin, Kristian

Christopher (Greek) "Christ-bearer." Religious: the name honors St. Christopher.
Chris, Chrissie, Chrissy, Christoffer, Christoforo, Christoper, Christoph, Christophe, Christophorus, Cris, Cristobál, Cristoforo, Christos, Kit, Kristo, Kristofer, Kristofor, Kristoforo, Kristos

Chuck a familiar form of Charles.

Cicero (Latin) "chickpea." Historical: a famous Roman orator-statesman.

Cid (Spanish) "a lord." Literary: El Cid was an 11th-century Spanish hero and soldier of fortune.
Cyd

Clare (Latin) "famous." A short form of Clarence.
Clair

Clarence (Latin) "bright; famous."
Clair, Clarance, Clare

Clark (Old French) "scholar."
Clarke, Clerc, Clerk

Claude (Latin) "lame."
Claudell, Claudian, Claudianus, Claudio, Claudius, Claus

Clay (Old English) "from the earth." A short form of Clayborne; Clayton.

Clayborne (Old English) "born of the earth."
Claiborn, Claiborne, Clay, Clayborn, Claybourne

Clayton (Old English) "from the farm built on clay."

Clement (Latin) "merciful." Biblical: a disciple of Paul.
Clem, Clemens, Clemente, Clementius, Clemmie, Clemmy, Clim, Klemens, Klement, Kliment

Cleon (Greek) "famous."
Kleon

Cletus (Greek) "summoned."
Cletis

Cleveland (Old English) "from the cliffs." See also Clive.
Cleavland, Cleve, Clevey, Clevie

Cliff (Old English) "steep rock, cliff." A short form of Clifford. See also Clive.

Clifford (Old English) "from the cliff at the river crossing."
Cliff

Clifton (Old English) "from the town near the cliffs."
Cliff, Clift

Clint a short form of Clinton.

Clinton (Old English) "from the headland farm."
Clint

Clive (Old English) "from the cliff." See also Cleveland; Cliff.
Cleve, Clyve

Clyde (Scottish Gaelic) "rocky eminence; heard from afar"; (Welsh) "warm."
Cly, Clywd

Cody (Old English) "a cushion." Historical: the name honors "Buffalo Bill" Cody.
Codi, Codie

Colbert (Old English) "outstanding seafarer."
Cole, Colt, Colvert, Culbert

Colby (Old English) "from the black farm."
Cole

Cole a familiar form of Nicholas. A short form of names beginning with the sound "cole."

Coleman (Old English) "adherent of Nicholas."
Cole, Colman

Colin (Irish Gaelic) "child." A familiar form of Nicholas.
Cailean, Colan, Cole, Collin

Collier (Old English) "miner."
Colier, Colis, Collayer, Collis, Collyer, Colyer

Colton (Old English) "from the coal town."
Colt

Conan (Old English) "intelligent." See also Channing.
Con, Conant, Conn, Conney, Connie, Conny

Conlan (Irish Gaelic) "hero."
Con, Conlen, Conley, Conlin, Conn, Conney, Connie, Conny

Connor (Irish Gaelic) "wise aid."

Conrad (Old German) "honest counselor."
Con, Conn, Conney, Connie, Conny, Conrade, Conrado, Cort, Koenraad, Konrad, Kort, Kurt

Conroy (Irish Gaelic) "wise man."
Con, Conn, Conney, Connie, Conny, Roy

Constantine (Latin) "firm; constant." Historical: one of the greatest Roman emperors.
Con, Conn, Conney, Connie, Conny, Constantin, Constantino, Costa, Konstantin, Konstantine

Conway (Irish Gaelic) "hound of the plain."
Con, Conn, Conney, Connie, Conny

Cooper (Old English) "barrelmaker."
Coop

Corbett (Latin) "raven."
Corbet, Corbie, Corbin, Corby, Cory

Cordell (Old French) "ropemaker."
Cord, Cordie, Cordy, Cory

Corey (Irish Gaelic) "from the hollow."
Cori, Correy, Corrie, Cory, Korey, Kory

Cornelius (Latin) "horn-colored; having horn-colored hair."
Conney, Connie, Conny, Cornall, Cornell, Corney, Cornie, Corny, Cory, Neel, Nelly

Cornell a French form of Cornelius.
Cornall, Corney, Cornie, Corny, Cory

Cort (Old German) "bold"; (Scandinavian) "short." See also Conrad; Courtney; Curtis.
Cortie, Corty, Kort

Cory a short form of names beginning with "cor."

Corydon (Greek) "lark." See also Cory.
Coridon, Cory, Coryden

Cosmo (Greek) "order, harmony; the universe."
Cos, Cosimo, Cosmé, Cozmo

Courtland (Old English) "from the farmstead or court land."
Court

Courtney (Old French) "from the court." See also Conrad; Cort; Curtis.
Cort, Court, Courtnay, Curt

Cowan (Irish Gaelic) "hillside hollow."
Coe, Cowey, Cowie

Craig (Irish Gaelic) "from near the crag."
Craggie, Craggy

Crandall (Old English) "from the cranes' valley."
Cran, Crandell

Crawford (Old English) "from the ford of the crow."
Craw, Crow, Ford

Creighton (Old English) "from the estate near the creek."
Creigh, Creight, Crichton

Crispin (Latin) "curly haired."

Cromwell (Old English) "dweller by the winding brook."

Crosby (Scandinavian) "from the shrine of the cross."
Cross

Cullen (Irish Gaelic) "handsome."
Cull, Cullan, Culley, Cullie, Cullin, Cully

Culver (Old English) "dove."
Colver, Cull, Cullie, Cully

Curran (Irish Gaelic) "hero."
Curr, Currey, Currie, Curry

Curt a short form of Courtney; Curtis. See also Conrad.
Kurt

Curtis (Old French) "courteous." See also Conrad; Courtney.
Curcio, Curt, Curtice, Kurtis

Cutler (Old English) "knifemaker."
Cut, Cuttie, Cutty

Cy a short form of Cyril; Cyrus.

Cyril (Greek) "lordly."
Cirillo, Cirilo, Cy, Cyrill, Cyrille, Cyrillus

Cyrus (Persian) "sun." Historical: Cyrus the Great was a Persian emperor.
Ciro, Cy, Russ

Dacey (Irish Gaelic) "southerner."
Dace, Dacy

Dag (Scandinavian) "day or brightness." Historical: Dag Hammerskjold, former secretary general of the United Nations.
Dagny

Dale (Old English) "from the valley."
Dael, Dal

Dallas (Irish Gaelic) "wise."
Dal, Dall, Dallis

Dalston (Old English) "from Daegal's place."
Dalis, Dallon

Dalton (Old English) "from the estate in the valley."
Dal, Dalt, Tony

Damek (Slavic) "man of the earth." A Slavic form of Adam.
Adamec, Adamek, Adamik, Adamok, Adham, Damick, Damicke

Damian a German form of Damon.

Damon (Greek) "constant; tamer."
Dame, Damian, Damiano, Damien

Dan a short form of Daniel; Riordan.
Dannie, Danny

Dana (Scandinavian) "from Denmark."
Dane

Dane (Old English) "from Denmark."
Danie

Daniel (Hebrew) "God is my judge." Biblical: a great Hebrew prophet.
Dan, Dani, Dannel, Dannie, Danny

Dante (Latin) "lasting."

Darby (Irish Gaelic) "free man"; (Old Norse) "from the deer estate."
Dar, Darb, Darbee, Derby

Darcy (Irish Gaelic) "dark "
D'Arcy, Dar, Darce

Darius (Greek) "wealthy."
Dare, Dario, Derry

Darnell (Old English) "from the hidden place."
Dar, Darn, Darnall

Darrel (French) "beloved."
Dare, Darrell, Darrill, Darryl, Daryl, Daryle, Derril

Darren (Irish Gaelic) "great." A familiar form of Dorian.
Dare, Daren, Darin, Daron, Darrin, Derron

Darwin (Old English) "beloved friend."
Derwin

Dave a short form of David; Davis.
Davie, Davy

David (Hebrew) "beloved." Biblical: the first King of Israel.
Dav, Dave, Davey, Davidde, Davide, Davidson, Davie, Davin, Davis, Daven, Davon, Davy, Dov

Davis (Old English) "son of David."
Dave, Davie, Davy

Dean (Old English) "from the valley."
Deane, Dene, Dino

Dedrick (Old German) "ruler of people."
Dedric

Delaney (Irish Gaelic) "descendant of the challenger."
Delainey

Delano (Old French) "of the night."

Delbert (Old English) "bright as day."
Bert, Bertie, Berty, Del

Delmore (Old French) "from the sea."
Del, Delmar, Delmer, Delmor

Delwin (Old English) "proud friend."
Del, Delwyn

Demetrius (Greek) "belonging to Demeter (goddess of fertility)."
Demetre, Demetri, Demetris, Dimitri, Dimitry, Dmitri

Dempsey (Irish Gaelic) "proud."
Demp

Denby (Scandinavian) "from the village of the Danes."
Danby, Den, Denney, Dennie, Denny

Dennis (Greek) "of Dionysus (god of wine and vegetation)."
Den, Denis, Dennet, Denney, Dennie, Dennison, Denny, Denys, Dion, Dionisio, Dionysus, Ennis

Dennison (Old English) "son of Dennis."
Den, Denison, Dennie, Denny

Denny a short form of names beginning with "den."
Den, Denney, Dennie

Denton (Old English) "from the valley estate."
Den, Denney, Dennie, Denny, Dent, Denten

Denver (Old English) "green valley."

Derek (Old German) "ruler of the people." A short form of Theodoric.
Darrick, Derick, Derrek, Derrick, Derrik, Derk, Dirk

Dermot (Irish Gaelic) "free from envy."
Der, Dermott, Diarmid

Derrick a form of Derek.

Derry (Irish Gaelic) "red-haired."
Dare

Desmond (Irish Gaelic) "man from south Munster."
Des, Desi, Desmund

Devin (Irish Gaelic) "poet."
Dev, Devy

Devlin (Irish Gaelic) "brave; fierce."
Dev, Devland, Devlen

Dewey (Welsh) "prized."
Dew, Dewie

De Witt (Flemish) "blond."
DeWitt, Dewitt, Dwight, Wit, Wittie, Witty

Dexter (Latin) "dexterous."
Decca, Deck, Dex

Dick a short form of Richard.
Dickie, Dicky

Diego a Spanish form of James.

Dietrich a German form of Theodoric.

Dillon (Irish Gaelic) "faithful." See also Dylan.
Dill, Dillie, Dilly

Dinsmore (Irish Gaelic) "from the fortified hill."
Dinnie, Dinny, Dinse

Dirk a short form of Derek; Theodoric.

Dmitri a Russian form of Demetrius.

Dolf, Dolph short forms of Adolph.

Dominic (Latin) "belonging to the Lord."
Dom, Domenic, Domenico, Domingo, Dominick, Dominik, Dominique, Nick, Nickie, Nicky

Don a short form of names beginning with "don."
Donn, Donnie, Donny

Donahue (Irish Gaelic) "dark warrior."
Don, Donn, Donnie, Donny, Donohue

Donald (Irish Gaelic) "world ruler."
Don, Donal, Donall, Donalt, Donaugh, Donn, Donnell, Donnie, Donny

Donnelly (Irish Gaelic) "brave dark man."
Don, Donn, Donnell, Donnie, Donny

Donovan (Irish Gaelic) "dark warrior."
Don, Donavon, Donn, Donnie, Donny

Doran (Hebrew-Greek) "gift."
Dore, Dorian, Dorran, Dorren

Dorian (Greek) "from the sea." See also Dory; Isidore.
Darren, Dore, Dorey, Dorie, Dory

Doug a short form of Douglas.
Dougie, Dougy

Douglas (Scottish Gaelic) "from the dark water."
Doug, Dougie, Douglass, Dougy, Dugaid

Dov a Hebrew short form of David.

Dovev (Hebrew) "to whisper."
Dov

Doyle (Irish Gaelic) "dark stranger."
Doy

Drake (Middle English) "owner of the 'Sign of the Dragon' inn."

Drew (Old French) "sturdy"; (Old Welsh) "wise." A short form of Andrew.
Dru, Drud, Drugi

Dryden (Old English) "from the dry valley."
Dry

Duane (Irish Gaelic) "little and dark."
Dewain, Dwain, Dwayne

Dudley (Old English) "from the people's meadow."
Dud

Duff (Celtic) "dark."
Duffie, Duffy

Duke (Old French) "leader; duke."
Dukey, Dukie, Duky

Duncan (Scottish Gaelic) "dark-skinned warrior."
Dun, Dunc, Dunn

Dunham (Celtic) "dark man."

Dunstan (Old English) "from the brown stone hill or fortress."
Dun

Durant (Latin) "enduring."
Dante, Durand, Durante

Durward (Old English) "gatekeeper; doorward."
Derward, Dur, Ward

Dustin (Old German) "valiant fighter."
Dust, Dustan, Dustie, Duston, Dusty

Dwayne a form of Duane.

Dwight a modern English form of De Witt.

Dylan (Old Welsh) "from the sea." See also Dillon.
Dilan, Dill, Dillie, Dilly

Eamon an Irish form of Edmund.

Earl (Old English) "nobleman."
Earle, Earlie, Early, Erl, Erle, Errol, Erroll, Rollo

Eaton (Old English) "from the estate on the river."
Eatton

Ebenezer (Hebrew) "stone of help."
Eb, Eben, Ebeneser

Ed a short form of names beginning with "ed."
Edan, Eddie, Eddy

Eden (Hebrew) "delight." Biblical: the garden of Adam and Eve.
Ed

Edgar (Old English) "successful spearman."
Ed, Eddie, Eddy, Edgard, Edgardo, Ned, Neddie, Neddy, Ted, Teddie, Teddy

Edison (Old English) "son of Edward."
Ed, Eddie, Eddy, Edson

Edmund (Old English) "prosperous protector."
Eadmund, Eamon, Ed, Edd, Eddie, Edmon, Edmond, Edmondo, Ned, Neddie, Neddy, Ted, Teddie, Teddy

Edsel (Old English) "from the rich man's house."
Ed, Eddie, Eddy

Edward (Old English) "happy protector." Historical: the name of many English kings.
Ed, Eddie, Eddy, Edik, Édouard, Eduard, Eduardo, Edvard, Ewart, Lalo, Ned, Neddie, Neddy, Ted, Teddie, Teddy

Edwin (Old English) "rich friend."
Ed, Eddie, Eddy, Edlin, Eduino, Ned, Neddie, Neddy, Ted, Teddie, Teddy

Efrem a modern form of Ephraim.

Egan (Irish Gaelic) "ardent, fiery."
Egon

Egbert (Old English) "bright as a sword."
Bert, Bertie, Berty

Elden, Eldon forms of Alden. See also Elton.

Eldred (Old English) "sage counsel."
Aldred, Eldrid

Eldridge a form of Aldrich. See also Eldred.
El, Eldredge

Eleazar (Hebrew) "God has helped." See also Lazarus.
Elazaro, Eléazar, Eli, Elie, Eliezer, Ely

Eli (Hebrew) "height." A short form of Eleazar; Elijah; Elisha. Biblical: the high priest who trained the prophet Samuel.
Ely

Elias a Greek form of Elijah.

Elijah (Hebrew) "Jehovah is God." Biblical: a great Hebrew prophet.
El, Eli, Elia, Elias, Elihu, Eliot, Elliott, Ellis, Ely

Elisha (Hebrew) "the Lord is salvation." Biblical: a prophet, successor to Elijah.
Eli, Elisée, Eliseo, Elish, Ely, Lisha

Ellard (Old German) "nobly brave."

Ellery (Old English) "from the elder tree island."
Ellary, Ellerey

Elliott a modern English form of Elijah.
Eliot, Eliott, Elliot

Ellis a modern form of Elijah (from Elias).

Ellison (Old English) "son of Ellis."
Elson

Ellsworth (Old English) "nobleman's estate."
Ellswerth, Elsworth

Elmer (Old English) "noble; famous." See also Elmo.
Aylmar, Aylmer, Aymer

Elmo (Italian) "helmet; protector." A familiar form of Anselm. See also Elmer.
Elmore

Elroy a form of Leroy.

Elston (Old English) "nobleman's town."

Elton (Old English) "from the old town."
Alden, Aldon, Eldon

Elvis (Scandinavian) "allwise." A form of Elwin.
Al, Alvis, El

Elwin (Old English) "friend of the elves."
El, Elvin, Elvis, Elvyn, Elwyn, Win, Winnie, Winny

Elwood (Old English) "from the old wood."
Ellwood, Woody

Emerson (Old German-English) "son of the industrious ruler." See also Emery.

Emery (Old German) "industrious ruler."
Amerigo, Amery, Amory, Emmerich, Emmerie, Emmery, Emory

Emil (Latin) "flattering, winning."
Emelen, Émile, Emilio, Emlen, Emlyn

Emlyn a Welsh form of Emil.
Emelen, Emlen, Emlin

Emmanuel (Hebrew) "God is with us."
Emanuel, Emanuele, Immanuel, Mannie, Manny, Manuel

Emmett a surname formed from Emma, used as a first name to honor Robert Emmett, Irish patriot.
Em, Emmet, Emmit, Emmott, Emmy

Engelbert (Old German) "bright as an angel."
Bert, Bertie, Berty, Englebert, Ingelbert, Inglebert

Enoch (Hebrew) "dedicated; consecrated." Biblical: the father of Methuselah.

Enos (Hebrew) "man."

Enrico an Italian form of Henry.

Ephraim (Hebrew) "very fruitful." Biblical: the second son of Joseph.
Efrem, Efren, Ephrem

Erasmus (Greek) "lovable." See also Erastus.
Erasme, Erasmo

Erastus (Greek) "beloved." See also Erasmus.
Eraste, Ras, Rastus

Erhard (Old German) "strong resolution."
Erhart

Eric (Scandinavian) "everruler; ever-powerful." A short form of Frederick. Historical: Eric the Red was a Viking hero.
Erek, Erich, Erick, Erik, Errick, Rick, Rickie, Ricky

Erin (Irish Gaelic) "peace."

Ernest (Old English) "earnest."
Ernesto, Ernestus, Ernie, Ernst, Erny

Errol a German form of Earl.
Erroll, Rollo

Erskine (Scottish Gaelic) "from the height of the cliff."
Kin, Kinnie, Kinny

Ervin, Erwin forms of Irving.

Esmond (Old English) "gracious protector."

Ethan (Hebrew) "firm."
Etan, Ethe

Étienne a French form of Stephen.

Eugene (Greek) "well-born."
Eugen, Eugéne, Eugenio, Eugenius, Gene

Eustace (Greek) "steadfast"; (Latin) "rich in corn."
Eustache, Eustashe, Eustasius, Eustatius, Eustazio, Eustis, Stacie, Stacy

Evan (Welsh) "young warrior." A Welsh form of John.
Ev, Even, Evin, Evyn, Ewan, Ewen, Owen

Evelyn a surname, often used as a masculine first name in England.
Evelin

Everett (Old English) "strong as a boar."
Eberhard, Ev, Everard, Evered, Eward, Ewart

Ezekiel (Hebrew) "strength of God." Biblical: one of the Hebrew prophets.
Ezéchiel, Ezequiel, Eziechiele, Zeke

Ezra (Hebrew) "helper." Biblical: a prophet and leader of the Israelites.
Esdras, Esra, Ezri

Fabian (Latin) "bean grower."
Fabe, Faber, Fabiano, Fabien, Fabio

Fairfax (Old English) "fair-haired."
Fair, Fax

Falkner (Old English) "trainer of falcons."
Faulkner, Fowler

Farley (Old English) "from the bull or sheep meadow."
Fairleigh, Fairlie, Far, Farlay, Farlee, Farleigh, Farlie, Farly

Farrell (Irish Gaelic) "heroic."
Farr, Farrel, Ferrel, Ferrell

Favian (Latin) "a man of understanding."

Felix (Latin) "fortunate."
Fee, Felic, Félice, Felicio, Felike, Feliks, Felizio

Felton (Old English) "from the estate built on the meadow."
Felt, Felten, Feltie, Felty

Fenton (Old English) "from the marshland farm."
Fen, Fennie, Fenny

Ferdinand (Old German) "world-daring."
Ferd, Ferdie, Ferdy, Fergus, Fernando, Hernando

Fergus (Irish Gaelic) "strong man." An Irish form of Ferdinand.
Ferguson

Fermin (Spanish) "firm, strong."
Firmin

Ferris (Irish Gaelic) "Peter, the Rock." An Irish form of Peter (from Pierce).
Farris

Fidel (Latin) "faithful."
Fidèle, Fidelio

Fielding (Old English) "from the field."
Fee, Field

Filbert (Old English) "brilliant."
Bert, Filberte, Filberto, Phil, Philbert

Filmore (Old English) "very famous."
Filmer, Phil

Finlay (Irish Gaelic) "little fair-haired soldier."
Fin, Findlay, Findley, Finley, Finn

Finn (Irish Gaelic) "fair-haired and fair-complected"; (Old German) "from Finland." A short form of Finlay.
Finnie, Finny

Fitz (Old English) "son." A short form of names beginning with "fitz."

Fitzgerald (Old English) "son of the spearmighty." See also Gerald.
Fitz, Gerald, Gerrie, Gerry, Jerry

Fitzhugh (Old English) "son of the intelligent man." See also Hugh.
Fitz, Hugh

Fitzpatrick (Old English) "son of a nobleman." See also Patrick.
Fitz, Pat, Patrick

Flavian (Latin) "blonde, yellow-haired."
Flavio, Flavius

Fleming (Old English) "dutchman."
Flem, Flemming

Fletcher (Middle English) "arrow-featherer, fletcher."
Fletch

Flint (Old English) "stream."

Florian (Latin) "flowering or blooming."
Flory

Floyd an English form of Lloyd.

Flynn (Irish Gaelic) "son of the red-haired man."
Flin, Flinn

Forbes (Irish Gaelic) "prosperous."

Ford (Old English) "river crossing." A short form of names ending in "ford."

Forest, Forrest (Old French) "forest; woodsman."
Forester, Forrester, Forster, Foss, Foster

Fortuné (Old French) "lucky."
Fortunato, Fortune, Fortunio

Foster (Latin) "keeper of the woods." A form of Forrest.

Fowler (Old English) "trapper of wild fowl."
Falconer, Falkner

Francis (Latin) "Frenchman." Religious: the name honors St. Francis of Assisi. See also Franklin.
Chico, Fran, Francesco, Franchot, Francisco, Franciskus, François, Frank, Frankie, Franky, Frannie, Franny, Frans, Fransisco, Frants, Franz, Franzen, Frasco, Frasquito, Paco, Pacorro, Panchito, Pancho, Paquito

François a French form of Francis.

Frank a short form of Francis; Franklin.
Frankie, Franky

Franklin (Middle English) "free landowner." See also Francis.
Fran, Francklin, Francklyn, Frank, Frankie, Franklyn, Franky

Frazer (Old English) "curly-haired"; (Old French) "strawberry."
Fraser, Frasier, Fraze, Frazier

Fred a short form of names containing "fred."
Freddie, Freddy

Frederick (Old German) "ruler in peace."
Eric, Erich, Erick, Erik, Federico, Fred, Freddie, Freddy, Fredek, Frédéric, Frederich, Frederico, Frederigo, Frederik, Fredric, Fredrick, Friedrich, Friedrick, Fritz, Ric, Rick, Rickie, Ricky

Freeborn (Old English) "child of freedom."
Free, Born, Bornie

Freeman (Old English) "free man."
Free, Freedman, Freeland, Freemon

Fremont (Old German) "guardian of freedom."
Free, Monty

Fritz a German familiar form of Frederick.

Fulton (Old English) "a field near the town."

Fulbright (Old German) "very bright."
Fulbert, Philbert

Fuller (Old English) "one who shrinks and thickens cloth."

Gabriel (Hebrew) "devoted to God." Biblical: the Archangel of the Annunciation.
Gabbie, Gabby, Gabe, Gabi, Gabie, Gabriele, Gabriello, Gaby

Gage (Old French) "pledge."

Gale (Irish Gaelic) "stranger"; (Old English) "gay, lively." A short form of Galen.
Gael, Gail, Gaile, Gayle

Galen (Irish Gaelic) "intelligent."
Gaelan, Gale, Gayle

Gallagher (Irish Gaelic) "eager helper."

Galvin (Irish Gaelic) "sparrow."
Gal, Galvan, Galven

Gamal, Gamali (Arabic) "camel."
Jamaal, Jammal

Gannon (Irish Gaelic) "fair-complected."
Gan, Gannie, Ganny

Gardner (Middle English) "gardener."
Gar, Gard, Gardener, Gardie, Gardiner, Gardy

Gareth (Welsh) "gentle." See also Garrett.
Gar, Garth

Garfield (Old English) "battlefield."
Field, Gar

Garland (Old English) "from the battlefield"; (Old French) "wreath."
Gar, Garlen

Garner (Old French) "armed sentry."
Gar

Garnett (Old English) "armed with a spear"; (Latin) "pomegranate seed; garnet stone."
Gar, Garnet

Garrett (Old English) "with a mighty spear." See also Gareth; Garth.
Gar, Garrard, Garret, Garreth, Garrot, Garrott, Jarret, Jarrett

Garrick (Old English) "oak spear."
Garek, Garik, Garrek, Garrik

Garth (Scandinavian) "grounds keeper." See also Gareth; Garrett.

Garvey (Irish Gaelic) "rough peace."
Garv, Garvy

Garvin (Old English) "comrade in battle."
Gar, Garwin, Vin, Vinnie, Vinny, Win, Winnie, Winny

Garwood (Old English) "from the fir tree forest."
Gar, Wood, Woodie, Woody

Gary (Old English) "spear-carrier." A familiar form of Gerald.
Gare, Garey, Garry

Gaspar a French form of Casper.
Gaspard

Gaston (French) "man from Gascony."

Gavin (Welsh) "white hawk."
Gav, Gavan, Gaven, Gawain, Gawen

Gaylord (Old French) "gay lord; jailer (gaoler)."
Gallard, Gay, Gayelord, Gayler, Gaylor

Gaynor (Irish Gaelic) "son of the fair-complected man."
Gainer, Gainor, Gay, Gayner

Gene a familiar form of Eugene.

Geno an Italian form of John.
Jeno

Geoffrey an English form of Godfrey; Jeffrey.
Geoff, Geoffry, Jeff

George (Greek) "farmer."
Egor, Georas, Geordie, Georg, Georges, Georgie, Georgy, Giorgio, Goran, Jorgan, Jorge, Yurik

Gerald (Old German) "spearruler." See also Gerard.
Garald, Garold, Gary, Gearalt, Gearard, Gerard, Gerek, Gerick, Gerik, Gérrard, Gerri, Gerrie, Gerry, Giraldo, Giraud, Jerald, Jerrie, Jerrold, Jerry

Gerard (Old English) "spearhard." See also Gerald.
Gearard, Gerardo, Géraud, Gerhard, Gerhardt, Gerrard, Gerri, Gerrie, Gerry, Gherardo

Germain (Middle English) "sprout, bud."
Germaine, Germayne, Jermain, Jermaine, Jermayne

Gershom (Hebrew) "exile."
Gersham

Gervase (Old German) "honorable."
Garvey, Gervais, Jarv, Jarvey

Giacomo an Italian form of Jacob.
Giacamo, Giamo, Gian

Gideon (Hebrew) "feller of trees; destroyer." Biblical: a judge who delivered the Israelites from captivity.

Gifford (Old English) "bold giver."
Giff, Giffard, Gifferd, Giffie, Giffy

Gilbert (Old English) "trusted."
Bert, Bertie, Berty, Burt, Burtie, Burty, Gib, Gibb, Gibbie, Gibby, Gil, Gilberto, Gilburt, Gill, Giselbert, Guilbert, Wilbert, Wilbur, Wilburt, Will

Gilchrist (Irish Gaelic) "servant of Christ."
Gil, Gill, Gillie, Gilly

Giles (Greek) "shield bearer."
Egide, Egidio, Egidius, Gide, Gil, Gill, Gilles

Gilmore (Irish Gaelic) "devoted to the Virgin Mary."
Gil, Gill, Gillie, Gillmore, Gilly, Gilmour

Gilroy (Irish Gaelic) "devoted to the king."
Gil, Gill, Gillie, Gilly, Roy

Gino an Italian short form of Ambrose (from Ambrogino) or Louis (from Luigino).

Giovanni an Italian form of John.
Gian, Gianni

Giuseppe an Italian form of Joseph.

Gladwin (Old English) "cheerful."
Glad, Gladdie, Gladdy, Win, Winnie, Winny

Glen, Glenn (Irish Gaelic) "valley." A short form of Glendon.
Glyn, Glynn

Glendon (Scottish Gaelic) "from the glen-fortress."
Glen, Glenden, Glenn

Goddard (Old German) "divinely firm."
Godard, Godart, Goddart, Gothart

Godfrey a German form of Jeffrey (from Gottfried).
Geoff, Geoffrey, Godfree, Godfry

Godwin (Old English) "friend of God."
Godewyn, Goodwin, Win, Winnie, Winny

Gonzalo (Spanish) "wolf."
Gonsalve, Gonzales

Gordon (Old English) "hill of the plains."
Gordan, Gorden, Gordie, Gordy

Grady (Irish Gaelic) "noble, illustrious."
Gradeigh, Gradey

Graham (Old English) "the gray home."
Graehme, Graeme, Gram

Granger (Old English) "farmer."
Grange, Gray

Grant (French) "great." A short form of Grantland.
Grantham, Granthem, Grantley, Grenville

Grantland (Old English) "from the great plains."
Grant

Granville (Old French) "from the large town."
Gran, Grannie, Granny

Grayson (Old English) "son of a bailiff."
Gray, Greerson, Grey, Greyson, Son, Sonnie, Sonny

Greg a short form of Gregory.
Graig, Gregg

Gregor a Scottish form of Gregory.

Gregory (Latin) "watchman; watchful."
Graig, Greg, Gregg, Greggory, Grégoire, Gregoor, Gregor, Gregorio, Gregorius

Griffin (Latin) "griffin (a mythical beast)." See also Griffith.
Griff, Griffie, Griffy

Griffith (Welsh) "fierce chief; ruddy." See also Griffin.
Griff, Griffie, Griffy

Griswold (Old German) "from the gray forest."
Gris, Griz

Grover (Old English) "from the grove."
Grove

Guido a German, Italian, Spanish, or Swedish form of Guy.

Guillermo the Spanish form of William.

Gunther (Scandinavian) "battle army; warrior."
Gun, Gunnar, Gunner, Guntar, Gunter

Gustave (Scandinavian) "staff of the Goths." Historical: the name honors Swedish king Gustavus Adolphus.
Gus, Gustaf, Gustav, Gustavo, Gustavus

Guthrie (Irish Gaelic) "from the windy place"; (Old German) "war hero."
Guthrey, Guthry

Guy (French) "guide"; (Old German) "warrior."
Guido

Hadley (Old English) "from the heath."
Had, Hadlee, Hadleigh, Lee, Leigh

Hakeem (Arabic) "wise."
Hakim

Hakon (Scandinavian) "of the chosen race."
Haakon, Hak, Hakan, Hako

Hal a short form of Harold; Henry; names beginning with "hal."

Haldan (Scandinavian) "half-Danish."
Dan, Dannie, Danny, Don, Donnie, Donny, Hal, Halden, Halfdan

Hale (Old English) "hero." A short form of Haley.
Hal, Heall

Haley (Irish Gaelic) "ingenious."
Hailey, Haily, Hal, Hale, Haleigh, Lee, Leigh

Hall (Old English) "from the manor or hall."

Halsey (Old English) "from Hal's island."
Hal, Hallsy, Halsy

Halstead (Old English) "from the manor."
Hal, Halsted, Steady

Hamal (Arabic) "lamb."

Hamid (Arabic) "thanking God."

Hamilton (Old English) "from the proud estate."
Ham, Hamel, Hamil, Tony

Hamlet (Old French-German) "little home." Literary: a Shakespearean tragic hero.
Ham, Hamnet

Hamlin (Old French-German) "little home-lover."
Ham, Hamlen, Lin, Lynn

Hank a familiar form of Henry.

Hanley (Old English) "of the high meadow."
Hanleigh, Henleigh, Henley

Hans a Scandinavian form of John.

Harcourt (Old French) "fortified dwelling."
Court, Harry

Hardy (Old German) "bold and daring."

Harlan (Old English) "from the army-land; from the hares' land."
Harland, Harlen, Harlin

Harley (Old English) "from the long field; from the army-meadow."
Arley

Harlow (Old English) "from the rough hill or army-hill."
Arlo

Harmon an English form of Herman.

Harold (Scandinavian) "army-ruler."
Araldo, Hal, Harald, Harry, Herold, Herrick

Harper (Old English) "harp player."
Harp

Harrison (Old English) "son of Harry."
Harris

Harry (Old English) "soldier." A short form of Harold; Henry. See also Harrison.

Hart (Old English) "hart (male) deer." A short form of Hartley.
Hartwell, Harwell, Harwill

Hartley (Old English) "from the deer meadow."
Hart

Harvey (Old German) "army-warrior."
Harv, Hervé, Hervey

Hashim (Arabic) "destroyer of evil."
Hasheem

Hasin (Indian) "laughing."
Hasen, Hassin

Haskel (Hebrew) "understanding."
Haskell

Haslett (Old English) "from the hazel tree land."
Haze, Hazel, Hazlett

Hastings (Old English) "son of the stern man."
Hastie, Hasty

Havelock (Scandinavian) "sea battle."

Haven (Old English, Middle Dutch) "harbor, port."
Hagan, Hagen, Hogan

Hayden (Old English) "from the hedged valley."
Haydon

Hayes (Old English) "from the hedged place."

Hayward (Old English) "guardian of the hedged area."

Haywood (Old English) "from the hedged forest."
Heywood, Woodie, Woody

Heath (Middle English) "from the heath."

Hector (Greek) "steadfast." Historical: a legendary Trojan warrior hero.
Ettore

Henderson (Old English, Scottish) "son of Henry."

Henri a French form of Henry.

Henry (Old German) "ruler of an estate."
Enrico, Enrique, Hal, Hank, Harry, Heindrick, Heinrich, Heinrik, Hendrick, Hendrik, Henri, Henrik

Herbert (Old German) "glorious soldier."
Bert, Bertie, Berty, Eberto, Harbert, Hébert, Herb, Herbie, Herby, Heriberto

Hercules (Greek) "glorious gift." Mythological: a hero renowned for his Twelve Labors.
Herc, Hercule, Herculie

Herman (Latin) "high-ranking person"; (Old German) "warrior."
Armand, Armando, Armin, Ermanno, Ermin, Harman, Harmon, Hermann, Hermie, Hermon, Hermy

Hernando a Spanish form of Ferdinand.

Hershel (Hebrew) "deer."
Hersch, Herschel, Hersh, Hirsch

Hewett (Old French-German) "little and intelligent." See also Hugh.
Hew, Hewet, Hewie, Hewitt

Heywood a form of Haywood.

Hilary (Latin) "cheerful."
Hi, Hilaire, Hilario, Hilarius, Hill, Hillary, Hillery, Hillie, Hilly, Ilario

Hillard (Old German) "brave warrior."
Hill, Hillier, Hillyer

Hillel (Hebrew) "greatly praised." Religious: the name honors Rabbi Hillel, reputed originator of the Talmud.

Hilliard (Old German) "war guardian."
Hillard

Hilton (Old English) "from the town on the hill."

Hiram (Hebrew) "most noble."
Hi, Hy

Hobart (Old German) "bright mind." A form of Hubert.
Hobard, Hobey, Hobie, Hoebart

Hogan (Irish Gaelic) "youth."

Holbrook (Old English) "from the brook in the hollow."
Brook, Holbrooke

Holden (Old English) "from the hollow in the valley."

Hollis (Old English) "from the grove of holly trees."
Holly

Holmes (Middle English) "from the river islands."

Holt (Old English) "from the forest."

Homer (Greek) "promise." Literary: the name honors the renowned ancient poet.
Homère, Homerus, Omero

Horace (Latin) "keeper of the hours." Literary: the name honors the ancient Roman poet.
Horacio, Horatio, Horatius, Orazio

Horst (Old German) "a thicket."

Horton (Old English) "from the gray estate."
Hort, Horten, Orton

Hosea (Hebrew) "salvation." Biblical: a Hebrew prophet.
Hose, Hoseia

Houston (Old English) "hill town."

Howard (Old English) "watchman."
Howey, Howie, Ward

Howe (Old German) "high."
Howey, Howie

Howland (Old English) "from the hills."
Howey, Howie, Howlan

Hubert (Old German) "bright mind."
Bert, Bertie, Berty, Hobard, Hobart, Hube, Huberto, Huey, Hubie, Hugh, Hugibert, Hugo, Humberto, Ugo, Ulberto

Hugh (Old English) "intelligence." A short form of Hubert. See also Hewett.
Hewe, Huey, Hughie, Hugo, Hugues, Ugo

Hugo a Latinized form of Hugh.
Ugo

Hulbert (Old German) "brilliant grace."
Bert, Bertie, Berty, Burt, Hulbard, Hulburt, Hull

Humbert (Old German) "brilliant Hun."
Hum, Umberto

Humphrey (Old German) "peaceful Hun."
Hum, Humfrey, Humfrid, Humfried, Hump, Humph, Hunfredo, Onfre, Onfroi, Onofredo

Hunt (Old English) "hunt." A short form of names beginning with "hunt."

Hunter (Old English) "hunter."
Hunt

Huntington (Old English) "hunting estate."
Hunt, Huntingdon

Huntley (Old English) "hunter's meadow."
Hunt, Huntlee, Lee, Leigh

Hurley (Irish Gaelic) "seatide."
Hurlee, Hurleigh

Hussein (Arabic) "little and handsome."
Husain, Husein

Hutton (Old English) "from the house on the jutting ledge."
Hut, Hutt, Huttan

Huxley (Old English) "from Hugh's meadow."
Hux, Lee, Leigh

Hyatt (Old English) "from the high gate."
Hy

Hyman an English form of Chaim.
Hayyim, Hy, Hymie, Mannie, Manny

Iago a Spanish and Welsh form of James. Literary: the villain in Shakespeare's *Othello*.

Ian a Scottish form of John.
Iain

Ignatius (Greek) meaning unknown; (Latin) "fiery, ardent."
Iggie, Iggy, Ignace, Ignacio, Ignacius, Ignaz, Ignazio, Inigo

Igor a Russian form of Inger.

Ingemar (Scandinavian) "famous son." See also Inger.
Ingamar, Ingmar

Inger (Scandinavian) "son's army." See also Ingemar.
Igor, Ingar

Inglebert a form of Engelbert.

Ingram (Old English) "angel."
Inglis, Ingra, Ingrim

Innis (Irish Gaelic) "from the island."
Innes, Inness

Ira (Hebrew) "watchful."

Irving (Irish Gaelic) "beautiful"; (Old English) "sea friend." See also Arvin.
Earvin, Erv, Ervin, Erwin, Irv, Irvin, Irvine, Irwin, Irwinn

Irwin a form of Irving.
Irwinn

Isaac (Hebrew) "he laughs." Biblical: the son of Abraham and Sarah.
Ike, Ikey, Isaak, Isac, Isacco, Isak, Izaak, Izak

Isaiah (Hebrew) "God is my helper; salvation of God." Biblical: a great Hebrew prophet.
Isa, Isiah, Issiah

Isidore (Greek) "gift of Isis."
Dore, Dory, Isador, Isadore, Isidor, Isidoro, Isidro, Izzy

Israel (Hebrew) "ruling with the Lord; wrestling with the Lord." Historical: the nation of Israel takes its name from that given Jacob after his wrestling with the angel.

Ivan a Russian form of John. See also Ivar.

Ivar (Scandinavian) "archer." See also Ivan.
Ive, Iver, Ivor, Yvon, Yvor

Jacinto (Spanish) "hyacinth."

Jack a familiar form of Jacob; John. A short form of Jackson.
Jock, Jocko

Jackson (Old English) "son of Jack."
Jack, Jackie, Jacky

Jacob (Hebrew) "supplanter." Biblical: son of Abraham, brother of Esau.
Cob, Cobb, Cobbie, Cobby, Giacobo, Giacomo, Giacopo, Hamish, Iago, Jack, Jackie, Jacky, Jacobo, Jacques, Jaime, Jake, Jakie, Jakob, James, Jamesy, Jamey, Jamie, Jay, Jayme, Jim, Jimmie, Jimmy, Seamus, Seumas, Shamus

Jacques a French form of Jacob; James.

Jael (Hebrew) "to ascend."

Jaime a Spanish form of James.
Jayme, Jaymie

Jake a short form of Jacob.

Jamal (Arabic) "beauty." Also a form of Gamal.
Jamaal, Jammal

James an English form of Jacob (from Jaime). Biblical: one of the Twelve Apostles.
Diego, Giacomo, Hamish, Iago, Jacques, Jaime, Jameson, Jamesy, Jamey, Jamie, Jamison, Jay, Jayme, Jim, Jimmie, Jimmy, Seamus, Seumas, Shamus

Jamie a familiar form of James
Jaime, Jaimie, Jayme

Jamil (Arabic) "handsome."
Jamill

Jan a Dutch and Slavic form of John.
Janek, Janos

Jareb (Hebrew) "he will contend."
Jarib

Jared (Hebrew) "one who rules."
Jarad, Jarid, Jarrad, Jarred, Jarrett, Jarrid, Jarrod, Jerad

Jarek (Slavic) "January."
Janiuszck, Januarius, Januisz

Jarlath (Latin) "man of control."
Jarl, Jarlen

Jarrett a form of Garrett
Jarret

Jarvis (Old German) "keen with a spear."
Jervis

Jason (Greek) "healer." Mythological: the hero who led the Argonauts in search of the Golden Fleece.
Jase, Jasen, Jasun, Jay, Jayson

Jasper an English form of Casper (from Gaspar).

Jay (Old French) "blue jay." A familiar form of Jacob; James; Jason.
Jae, Jaye

Jean a French form of John.

Jed (Hebrew) "beloved of the Lord." A short form of Jedidiah.
Jedd, Jeddy, Jedediah, Jedidiah

Jedidiah (Hebrew) "beloved of the Lord." See also Jed.

Jeff a short form of Jefferson; Jeffrey. A familiar form of Geoffrey.

Jefferson (Old English) "son of Jeffrey." Historical: the name honors Thomas Jefferson, third U.S. president.
Jeff, Jeffie, Jeffy

Jeffrey (Old French) "heavenly peace."
Geoff, Geoffrey, Godfrey, Gottfried, Jeff, Jefferey, Jeffie, Jeffy, Jeffry

Jeremiah (Hebrew) "appointed by Jehovah." Biblical: a great Hebrew prophet. See also Jerome.
Jere, Jereme, Jeremias, Jeremy, Jerry

Jeremy a modern form of Jeremiah.
Jeramey, Jeramie, Jere, Jereme, Jeremie, Jeromy, Jerry

Jerome (Latin) "holy name." See also Jeremiah.
Gerome, Gerrie, Gerry, Hieronymus, Jere, Jereme, Jerrome, Jerry

Jerry a short form of Gerald; Jeremiah; Jeremy; Jerome.
Jere, Jerri

Jess a short form of Jesse.

Jesse (Hebrew) "God exists." Biblical: the father of David.
Jess, Jessee, Jessey, Jessie

Jesus (Hebrew) "God will help." Biblical: son of Mary and Joseph; founder of the Christian religion.
Chucho, Jecho

Jethro (Hebrew) "preeminence." Biblical: the father-in-law of Moses.
Jeth

Jim a short form of James.
Jimmie, Jimmy

Joab (Hebrew) "praise the Lord."

Joachim (Hebrew) "the Lord will judge."
Akim, Joaquin

Job (Hebrew) "the afflicted." Biblical: a book of the Bible. Job is an upright man who is tested and endures many afflictions.

Jock a familiar form of Jacob; John.
Jocko

Jody a familiar form of Joseph.
Jodi, Jodie

Joe a short form of Joseph.
Joey

Joel (Hebrew) "Jehovah is the Lord." Biblical: a Hebrew prophet.

John (Hebrew) "God is gracious." Biblical: the name honors John the Baptist and John the Evangelist. See also Jonathan.
Evan, Ewan, Ewen, Gian, Giavani, Giovanni, Hanan, Hans, Iain, Ian, Jack, Jackie, Jacky, Jan, Janos, Jean, Jens, Jock, Jocko, Johan, Johann, Johannes, Johnnie, Johnny, Johny, Jon, Jone, Juan, Owen, Sean, Shaughn, Shaun, Shawn, Zane

Jon a form of John. A short form of Jonathan.

Jonah (Hebrew) "dove." Biblical: the prophet who was swallowed by a whale.
Jonas

Jonas (Hebrew) "the doer."

Jonathan (Hebrew) "Jehovah gave." Biblical: the friend of David. See also John.
Johnathan, Johnathon, Jon, Jonathon, Yanaton

Jordan (Hebrew) "descending."
Giordano, Jared, Jerad, Jordon, Jory, Jourdain

José a Spanish form of Joseph.
Joseito, Pepe, Pepillo, Pepito

Joseph (Hebrew) "he shall add." Biblical: Joseph ruled in Egypt; also, the husband of Mary.
Che, Giuseppe, Iosep, Jo, Joe, Joey, José, Jozef

Josh a short form of Joshua.

Joshua (Hebrew) "Jehovah saves." Biblical: Joshua led the Israelites into the Promised Land. See also Josiah.
Josh, Joshia, Joshuah

Josiah (Hebrew) "Jehovah supports." See also Joshua.
Josias

Juan a Spanish form of John.

Judah (Hebrew) "praised."
Jud, Judas, Judd, Jude

Judd a modern form of Judah.

Jude (Latin) "right in the law." Biblical: author of one of the books of the Bible.

Jules a French form of Julius.
Jule

Julian (Latin) "belonging or related to Julius."

Julius (Greek) "youthful and downy-bearded." Historical: Julius Caesar was a great Roman emperor. See also Julian.
Giulio, Jule, Jules, Julie, Julio

Justin (Latin) "upright."
Giustino, Giusto, Justen, Justinian, Justino, Justis, Justus

K

Kalil (Arabic) "good friend."
Kahaleel, Kahlil

Kane (Irish Gaelic) "tribute."
Kain, Kaine, Kayne

Kareem (Arabic) "noble, exalted."
Karim

Karl a German form of Charles.
Kale, Kalle, Karlan, Karlens, Karlik, Karlis

Karsten (Greek) "anointed."

Keane (Old English) "sharp, keen." See also Keenan.
Kean, Keen, Keene

Kearney a form of Carney.
Karney

Keefe (Irish Gaelic) "cherished; handsome."

Keegan (Irish Gaelic) "little and fiery."

Keenan (Irish Gaelic) "little and ancient." See also Keane.
Keen, Kienan

Keir (Celtic) "dark-skinned." See also Kerr.

Keith (Welsh) "from the forest"; (Scottish Gaelic) "from the battle place."

Kelby (Old German) "from the farm by the spring."
Keelby, Kelbee, Kellby

Kelly (Irish Gaelic) "warrior."
Kele, Kellen, Kelley

Kelsey (Scandinavian) "from the ship-island."

Kelton (Old English) "keel town; town where ships are built."
Keldon, Kelson

Kelvin (Old English) "lover of ships."
Kelwin

Ken a short form of names containing "ken."
Kenn, Kennie, Kenny

Kendall (Old English) "from the bright valley."
Ken, Kendal, Kendell, Kenn, Kennie, Kenny

Kendrick (Irish Gaelic) "son of Henry"; (Old English) "royal ruler."
Ken, Kendricks, Kenn, Kennie, Kenny, Rick, Rickie, Ricky

Kenley (Old English) "from the royal meadow."
Kenleigh

Kenn (Welsh) "clear water." A short form of names beginning with "ken."
Ken, Kennan, Kennie, Kenny, Kenon

Kennedy (Irish Gaelic) "helmeted chief." Historical: the name honors John F. Kennedy, thirty-fifth U.S. president.
Ken, Kenn, Kennie, Kenny

Kenneth (Irish Gaelic) "handsome"; (Old English) "royal oath."
Ken, Kenn, Kennet, Kennett, Kennie, Kennith, Kenny

Kent (Welsh) "white, bright." A short form of Kenton.
Ken, Kenn, Kennie, Kenny

Kenton (Old English) "from the king's estate."
Ken, Kenn, Kennie, Kenny, Kent

Kenyon (Irish Gaelic) "white-haired, blond."
Ken, Kenn, Kennie, Kenny

Kermit (Irish Gaelic) "free man."
Ker, Kermie, Kermy, Kerr

Kerr (Scandinavian) "marshland."
Carr

Kerry (Irish Gaelic) "dark; dark-haired."
Keary

Kerwin (Old English) "friend of the marshlands."
Kerwinn

Kevin (Irish Gaelic) "gentle, lovable."
Kev, Kevan, Keven, Kevon

Khalil (Arabic) "friend."

Kieran (Irish Gaelic) "little and dark-skinned."
Kiernan

Killian (Irish Gaelic) "little and warlike."
Kilian, Killie, Killy

Kim (Old English) "chief, ruler." A short form of Kimball.
Kimmie, Kimmy

Kimball (Old English) "warrior chief; royal and bold."
Kim, Kimbell, Kimble

Kincaid (Celtic) "battle chief."

King (Old English) "king." A short form of names beginning with "king."

Kingsley (Old English) "from the king's meadow."
King, Kingsley, Kingsly, Kinsley

Kingston (Old English) "from the king's estate."
King

Kipp (Old English) "from the pointed hill."
Kip, Kippar, Kipper, Kippie, Kippy

Kirby (Scandinavian) "from the church village."
Kerby

Kirk (Scandinavian) "from the church."
Kerk

Kit a familiar form of Christian; Christopher.

Knox (Old English) "from the hills."

Knute a Danish form of Canute.
Cnut, Knut

Koby a familiar form of Jacob.
Kobi

Kosey (African) "lion."
Kosse

Krishna (Hindi) "delightful."
Krisha, Krishnah

Kristopher a form of Christopher.
Kris, Kristofer, Kristoffer, Kristofor

Kurt a German form of Conrad.

Kwasi (African) "born on Sunday."

Kyle (Irish Gaelic) "handsome; from the strait."
Kiel, Kile, Kiley, Ky, Kylie

Ladd (Middle English) "attendant."
Lad, Laddie, Laddy

Laird (Scottish) "landed proprietor, laird."

Lamar (Old German) "famous throughout the land; famous as the land."
Lemar

Lambert (Old German) "bright land; bright as the land."
Bert, Bertie, Berty, Lamberto, Landbert

Lamont (Scandinavian) "lawyer."
Lammond, Lamond, Monty

Lance (Old German) "land."
Lancelot, Launce

Landon (Old English) "from the open, grassy meadow."
Landan

Lane (Middle English) "from the narrow road."
Laney, Lanie

Langdon (Old English) "from the long hill."
Landon, Langsdon, Langston

Langley (Old English) "from the long meadow."
Lang

Langston (Old English) "from the long, narrow town."
Langsdon

Lanny a short form of Orland; Roland.
Lannie, Lennie

Larry a familiar form of Lawrence.

Lars a Scandinavian form of Lawrence.

Latham (Scandinavian) "from the barn."
Laith, Lathe, Lay

Lathrop (Old English) "from the barn-farmstead."
Lathe, Lathrope, Lay

Latimer (Middle English) "interpreter."
Lat, Lattie, Latty

Lawford (Old English) "from the ford on the hill."
Ford, Law

Lawrence (Latin) "from Laurentium; laurel-crowned."
Larry, Lars, Lauren, Laurence, Laurens, Laurent, Laurie, Lauritz, Lawry, Lenci, Lon, Lonnie, Lonny, Lorant, Loren, Lorens, Lorenzo, Lorin, Lorrie, Lorry, Lowrance, Rance

Lawton (Old English) "from the estate on the hill."
Laughton, Law

Lazarus (Hebrew) "God will help." Biblical: Lazarus was raised from the dead. See also Eleazar.
Lazar, Lazare, Lazaro

Leander (Greek) "lionlike." See also Leonard.
Ander, Léandre, Leandro, Lee, Leigh, Leo

Lee (Old English) "from the meadow." A short form of names containing the sound "lee."
Leigh

Leif (Scandinavian) "beloved."
Lief

Leigh a form of Lee.

Leighton (Old English) "from the meadow farm."
Lay, Layton

Leland (Old English) "meadow land."
Lee, Leeland, Leigh

Lemuel (Hebrew) "devoted to the Lord."
Lem, Lemmie, Lemmy

Leo (Latin) "lion." A short form of Leander; Leonard; Leopold.
Lee, Léon, Lev, Lion, Lyon

Leon (French) "lion, lionlike." A French form of Leo. A short form of Leonard; Napoleon.

Leonard (Old German) "bold lion." See also Leander.
Lee, Len, Lenard, Lennard, Lennie, Lenny, Leo, Léon, Léonard, Leonardo, Leonerd, Leonhard, Leonid, Leonidas, Lonnard, Lonnie, Lonny

Leopold (Old German) "bold for the people."
Leo, Leupold

Leroy (Old French) "king."
Elroy, Lee, Leigh, Leroi, LeRoy, Roy

Les a short form of Leslie; Lester.

Leslie (Scottish Gaelic) "from the gray fortress."
Lee, Leigh, Les, Lesley, Lezlie

Lester (Latin) "from the chosen camp"; (Old English) "from Leicester."
Leicester, Les

Lev a Russian form of Leo.

Levi (Hebrew) "joined in harmony." Biblical: son of Jacob; name of the priestly tribe of Israel.
Levey, Levin, Levon, Levy

Lewis a short form of Llewellyn. A form of Louis.
Lew, Lewes, Lewie

Liam an Irish form of William.

Lincoln (Old English) "from the settlement by the pool." Historical: the name honors Abraham Lincoln, sixteenth U.S. president.
Linc, Link

Lindsay (Old English) "from the linden tree island."
Lind, Lindsey

Linus (Greek) "flaxenhaired."

Lionel (Old French) "lion cub." See also Leo.
Lionello

Livingston (Old English) "from Leif's town."

Llewellyn (Welsh) "lionlike; lightning."
Lew, Lewis, Llywellyn

Lloyd (Welsh) "grayhaired."
Floyd, Loy, Loydie

Locke (Old English) "from the forest."
Lock, Lockwood

Logan (Irish Gaelic) "from the hollow."

Lombard (Latin) "longbearded."
Bard, Barr

Lon, Lonnie, Lonny short forms of Alonzo; Lawrence.

London (Middle English) "fortress of the moon."

Loren a short form of Lawrence.
Lorin

Lorimer (Latin) "harness-maker."
Lorrie, Lorrimer, Lorry

Loring (Old German) "son of the famous warrior."
Lorrie, Lorry

Lorne a familiar form of Lawrence.
Lorn

Louis (Old German) "renowned warrior."
Aloysius, Lew, Lewis, Lou, Louie, Lucho, Ludvig, Ludwig, Luigi, Luis

Lowell (Old French) "little wolf."
Lovell, Lowe

Lucas a Danish, Dutch, German, or Irish form of Lucius; Luke.

Lucian (Latin) "shining, resplendent."
Luciano, Lucien

Lucius (Latin) "bringer of light." See also Lucian.
Luca, Lucais, Lucas, Luce, Lucias, Lucio, Lukas, Luke

Ludlow (Old English) "from the prince's hill." An English from of Ludwig.

Ludwig a German form of Louis.

Luis a Spanish form of Louis.

Luke (Greek) "from Lucania." A form of Lucius. Biblical: one of the Four Evangelists.
Lucais, Lucas, Lukas

Luther (Old German) "famous warrior." Religious: the name honors Martin Luther, Protestant reformer.
Lothaire, Lothario, Lutero

Lyle (Old French) "from the island."
Lisle, Ly, Lyell

Lyman (Old English) "a man from the meadow."

Lyndon (Old English) "from the linden tree hill."
Lin, Lindon, Lindy, Lyn, Lynn

Lynn (Old English) "waterfall; pool below a fall."
Lin, Linn, Lyn

Mac (Scottish Gaelic) "son of." A short form of names beginning with "mac"; "max"; "mc."
Mack

Mackenzie (Irish Gaelic) "son of the wise leader."
Mac, Mack

Macnair (Scottish Gaelic) "son of the heir."
Macknair

Madison (Old English) "son of the powerful soldier."
Maddie, Maddy, Son, Sonnie, Sonny

Magnus (Latin) "great."
Manus

Major (Latin) "greater."
Maje, Mayer, Mayor

Malachi (Hebrew) "angel."
Mal, Malachy

Malcolm (Scottish Gaelic) "follower of St. Columba (an early Scottish saint)."
Mal

Malik (Muslim) "master."

Mallory (Old German) "army counselor."
Mal

Malvin a form of Melvin.

Mandel (German) "almond."
Mannie, Manny

Manfred (Old English) "man of peace."
Fred, Freddie, Freddy, Mannie, Manny

Manuel a short form of Emmanuel.
Mano, Manolo

Marc a French form of Mark.

Marcel (Latin) "little and warlike."
Marcello, Marcellus, Marcelo

Marcus a form of Mark.

Mario an Italian form of Mark.

Marion a French form of Mary, usually reserved for boys.

Mark (Latin) "warlike." Biblical: one of the Four Evangelists.
Marc, Marco, Marcos, Marcus, Mario, Marius, Markos, Markus

Marlon (Old French) "little falcon." A familiar form of Merlin.
Marlin

Marlow (Old English) "from the hill by the lake."
Mar, Marlo, Marlowe

Marshall (Old French) "steward; horse-keeper."
Marsh, Marshal

Martin (Latin) "warlike."
Mart, Martainn, Marten, Martie, Martijn, Martino, Marty, Martyn

Marty a short form of Martin.

Marvin (Old English) "lover of the sea."
Marv, Marve, Marven, Marwin, Mervin, Merwin, Merwyn, Murvyn, Myrvyn, Myrwyn

Mason (Old French) "stoneworker."
Mace, Maison, Sonnie, Sonny

Matt a short form of Matthew.
Mattie, Matty

Matthew (Hebrew) "gift of the Lord." Biblical: one of the Four Evangelists.
Mata, Mateo, Mathe, Mathew, Mathian, Mathias, Matias, Matt, Matteo, Matthaeus, Matthäus, Mattheus, Matthias, Matthieu, Matthiew, Mattias, Mattie, Matty

Maurice (Latin) "dark-skinned." See also Moore; Morse. .
Mauricio, Maurie, Maurise, Maurits, Maurizio, Maury, Morey, Morie, Moritz, Morris

Max a short form of Maximilian; Maxwell.
Maxie, Maxy

Maximilian (Latin) "most excellent."
Mac, Mack, Massimiliano, Massimo, Max, Maxie, Maxim, Maximilianus, Maximilien, Maximo, Maxy

Maxwell (Old English) "from the influential man's well."
Mac, Mack, Max, Maxie, Maxy

Mayer a form of Major. See also Meyer.

Maynard (Old German) "powerful, brave."
May, Mayne, Ménard

Mead (Old English) "from the meadow."
Meade

Medwin (Old German) "strong friend."

Melbourne (Old English) "from the mill stream."
Mel, Melborn, Melburn

Melville (Old English-Old French) "from the estate of the hard worker."
Mel

Melvin (Irish Gaelic) "polished chief."
Mal, Malvin, Mel, Melvyn, Vin, Vinnie, Vinny

Mendel (East Semitic) "knowledge; wisdom."
Mendie, Mendy

Meredith (Welsh) "guardian from the sea."
Merideth, Merry

Merle (French) "blackbird." A short form of Merlin; Merrill.

Merlin (Middle English) "falcon." Literary: a famous wizard in Arthurian legend. See also Merrill.
Marlin, Marlon, Merle

Merrick (Old English) "ruler of the sea."

Merrill (Old French) "famous." See also Merlin.
Merill, Merle, Merrel, Merrell, Meryl

Merton (Old English) "from the town by the sea."
Merv, Merwyn, Murton

Mervin a form of Marvin.
Merwin, Merwyn

Meyer (German) "farmer"; (Hebrew) "bringer of light." See also Major.
Meier, Meir, Myer

Micah a Hebrew form of Michael. Biblical: a Hebrew prophet.
Mic, Mick, Mike, Mikey, Myca, Mycah

Michael (Hebrew) "who is like the Lord?"
Micah, Michail, Michal, Michale, Micheal, Michell, Michel, Michele, Mickey, Mickie, Micky, Miguel, Mikael, Mike, Mikel, Mikey, Mikkel, Mikol, Mischa, Mitch, Mitchel, Mitchell, Mychal

Mike a short form of Michael.
Mikey

Miles (Latin) "soldier"; (Old German) "merciful."
Milo, Myles

Millard (Latin) "caretaker of the mill."
Mill, Miller

Milo a German form of Miles.
Mylo

Milton (Old English) "from the mill town."
Milt, Miltie, Milty

Minor (Latin) "junior, younger." As Miner, an occupational name.
Miner

Mischa a Slavic form of Michael.

Mitch a short form of Mitchell.

Mitchell a Middle English form of Michael.
Mitch, Mitchel

Mohammed a form of Muhammad.

Monroe (Irish Gaelic) "from the mouth of the Roe River."
Monro, Munro, Munroe

Montague (French) "from the pointed mountain."
Monte, Monty

Monte (Latin) "mountain." A short form of Montague; Montgomery.

Montgomery (Old English) "from the rich man's mountain."
Monte, Monty

Monty a short form of names containing "mont."
Monti

Moore (Old French) "dark-complected." See also Maurice.

Mordecai (Hebrew) "belonging to Marduk" (the Babylonian creation god).
Mord, Mordy, Mort, Mortie, Morty

Morey a familiar form of Maurice; Morris; Morse; Seymour.
Morie, Morrie, Morry

Morgan (Scottish Gaelic) "from the edge of the sea."
Morgen, Morgun

Morley (Old English) "from the meadow on the moor."
Morlee, Morly

Morris an English form of Maurice.
Morey, Morie, Morrie, Morry

Morse (Old English) "son of Maurice."
Morey, Morie, Morrie, Morry

Mort a short form of Mordecai; Mortimer.
Mortie, Morty

Mortimer (Old French) "still water."
Mort, Mortie, Morty

Morton (Old English) "from the town near the moor."
Morten

Morven (Scottish Gaelic) "mariner."

Moses (Hebrew) "saved." Biblical: the Hebrew leader who brought the Ten Commandments down from Sinai.
Moe, Moise, Moisés, Mose, Moshe, Moss, Mozes

Moss a familiar form of Moses.

Muhammad (Arabic) "praised." Religious: Muhammad was the founder of the Muslim religion.
Hamid, Hammad, Mahmoud, Mahmud, Mohammed

Muir (Scottish Gaelic) "moor."

Murdock (Scottish Gaelic) "wealthy sailor."
Murdoch

Murray (Scottish Gaelic) "sailor."
Murry

Myron (Greek) "fragrant ointment."
My, Ron, Ronnie, Ronny

Napoleon (Greek) "lion of the woodland dell"; (Italian) "from Naples." Historical: the name honors Emperor Napoleon Bonaparte.
Leon, Nap, Napoléon, Nappie, Nappy

Nat, Nate short forms of Nathan; Nathaniel.

Nathan (Hebrew) "gift." A short form of Nathaniel. Biblical: a prophet who saved Solomon's kingdom.
Nat, Nate

Nathaniel (Hebrew) "gift of God." Biblical: one of the Twelve Apostles; he was also called Bartholomew.
Nat, Nataniel, Nate, Nathan, Nathanael, Nathanial, Natty

Neal an Irish form of Neil.
Nealy

Ned a familiar form of names beginning with "ed."
Neddie, Neddy

Nehemiah (Hebrew) "compassion of Jehovah." Biblical: a Hebrew prophet.

Neil (Irish Gaelic) "champion." Historical: Niall of the Nine Hostages, famous Irish ruler, founded the clan O'Neill.
Neal, Neale, Neall, Nealon, Neel, Neill, Neils, Nels, Nial, Niall, Niel, Niels, Nil, Niles, Nils

Nels a Scandinavian form of Neil; Nelson.

Nelson (English) "son of Neil."
Nealson, Neils, Nels, Niles, Nils, Nilson

Nero (Spanish, Latin) "stern."
Neron

Nestor (Greek) "traveler; wisdom."

Neville (Old French) "from the new town."
Nev, Nevil, Nevile

Nevin (Irish Gaelic) "worshipper of the saint"; (Old English) "nephew."
Nefen, Nev, Nevins, Niven

Newbold (Old English) "from the new building."

Newton (Old English) "from the new town."

Nicholas (Greek) "victory of the people." Religious: St. Nicholas is the patron of children.
Claus, Colas, Cole, Colet, Colin, Klaus, Niccolò, Nichole, Nichols, Nick, Nickey, Nickie, Nickolas, Nickolaus, Nicky, Nicol, Nicolai, Nicolas, Nicolis, Niki, Nikita, Nikki, Nikolai, Nikolas, Nikolaus, Nikolos, Nikos

Nick a short form of Nicholas.
Nickie, Nicky

Niels a Danish form of Neil; Nelson.
Niles, Nils

Nigel (Latin) "black."
Nye

Noah (Hebrew) "wandering; rest." Biblical: the patriarch who built the Ark.
Noach, Noak, Noé

Noble (Latin) "well-born."
Nobe, Nobie, Noby

Noel (French) "the Nativity; born at Christmas."
Natal, Natale, Noël, Nowell

Nolan (Irish Gaelic) "famous; noble."
Noland

Norbert (Scandinavian) "brilliant hero."
Bert, Bertie, Berty, Norbie, Norby

Norman (Old French) "Norseman."
Norm, Normand, Normie, Normy

Norris (Old French) "man from the north; nurse."
Norrie, Norry

Northrop (Old English) "from the north farm."
North, Northrup

Norton (Old English) "from the northern town."

Nuri (Hebrew) "fire."
Nur, Nuriel, Nuris

Nye (Middle English) "islander." A familiar form of Nigel.

Oakes (Old English) "from the oak trees."
Oak, Oakie, Oaks

Oakley (Old English) "from the oak-tree field."
Oak, Oakes, Oakie, Oakleii h, Oaks

Obadiah (Hebrew) "servant of God."
Obadias, Obed, Obediah, Obie, Oby

Odell (Scandinavian) "little and wealthy."
Dell, Ode, Odey, Odie, Ody

Ogden (Old English) "from the oak valley or hill."
Ogdan, Ogdon

Olaf (Scandinavian) "ancestral talisman." Historical: five Norwegian kings bore this name.
Olav, Ole, Olen, Olin

Olin an English form of Olaf.

Oliver (Latin) "olive tree"; (Scandinavian) "kind, affectionate."
Noll, Nollie, Nolly, Olivero, Olivier, Oliviero, Ollie, Olly, Olvan

Omar (Arabic) "first son; highest; follower of the Prophet."

Oren (Hebrew) "pine tree"; (Irish Gaelic) "pale-complected."
Oran, Orin, Orren, Orrin

Orestes (Greek) "mountain man." Mythological: a hero, son of Agamemnon.
Oreste

Orion (Greek) "son of fire." Mythological: a hunter who became the constellation of Orion.

Orland, Orlando (Old English) "from the pointed land." See also Roland.
Land, Lannie, Lanny, Orlan, Orlando

Orman (Old German) "mariner or shipman."
Ormand

Ormond (Old English) "from the bear mountain; spear-protector."

Orrin a form of Oren.
Orran, Orren

Orson (Latin) "bearlike."
Sonnie, Sonny, Urson

Orville (Old French) "from the golden estate."
Orv

Osborn (Old English) "warrior of God"; (Scandinavian) "divine bear."
Osborne, Osbourn, Osbourne, Ozzie, Ozzy

Oscar (Scandinavian) "divine spearman."
Oskar, Ossie, Ossy, Ozzie, Ozzy

Osgood (Old English) "divinely good."
Ozzie, Ozzy

Osmond (Old English) "divine protector."
Esme, Osmund, Ozzie, Ozzy

Oswald (Old English) "having power from God."
Ossie, Ossy, Oswell, Ozzie, Ozzy, Wald, Waldo

Otis (Old English) "son of Otto"; (Greek) "keen of hearing."
Oates, Otes

Otto (Old German) "rich."
Odo, Othello, Otho

Owen a form of Evan.
Ewen

Oxford (Old English) "from the river crossing of the oxen."
Ford

Ozzie a short form of names beginning with "os."
Ozzy

Pablo a Spanish form of Paul.

Paco (Italian) "to pack."

Paddy an Irish familiar form of Patrick (through Padriac).

Page (French) "youthful assistant."
Padget, Padgett, Paige

Palladin (North American Indian) "fighter."
Pallaten, Pallaton

Palmer (Old English) "palm-bearing pilgrim."
Palm

Park a short form of Parker.
Parke

Parker (Middle English) "guardian of the park."
Park, Parke

Parnell (Old French) "little Peter." Historical: the name honors the famous Irish politician, Charles Stewart Parnell.
Nell, Nellie, Nelly, Parrnell, Pernell

Parrish (Middle English) "from the churchyard."
Parrie, Parrisch, Parry

Parry a short form of Parrish. A form of Perry.

Pascal (Italian) "pertaining to Easter or Passover; born at Easter or Passover."
Pascale, Pace, Pasquale

Pat a short form of names containing "pat."
Pattie, Patty

Patrick (Latin) "nobleman." Religious: St. Patrick is the patron of Ireland.
Paddie, Paddy, Padraic, Padraig, Padriac, Pat, Paton, Patric, Patrice, Patricio, Patrizio, Patrizius, Patsy, Patten, Pattie, Patty

Patton (Old English) "from the warrior's estate."
Pat, Paten, Patin, Paton, Patten, Pattin, Patty

Paul (Latin) "small." Biblical: Saul, called Paul, was the great missionary and apostle of Christianity.
Pablo, Pall, Paolo, Paulie, Pauly, Pavel, Poul

Paxton (Latin) "from the peaceful town."
Packston, Paxon

Pedro a Spanish form of Peter.

Pembroke (Celtic) "from the headland."
Pembrook

Penn (Old English) "enclosure"; (Old German) "commander." A short form of Penrod.
Pennie, Penny

Penrod (Old German) "famous commander."
Pen, Penn, Pennie, Penny, Rod, Roddie, Roddy

Pepin (Old German) "petitioner; perseverant."
Pepi, Peppi, Peppie, Peppy

Percival (Old French) "pierce-the-valley." Literary: the name, invented by Chrétien de Troyes for the knight-hero of his epic about the Grail, also suggests "pierce-the-veil (of religious mystery)."
Parsifal, Perceval, Percy, Purcell

Percy (French) "from Percy." A short form of Percival.

Perry (Middle English) "pear tree"; (Old French) "little Peter." A familiar form of Peter.
Parry

Peter (Greek) "rock." Biblical: Simon (called Peter) was leader of the Twelve Apostles.
Farris, Ferris, Parry, Peadar, Pearce, Peder, Pedro, Peirce, Perkin, Perren, Perry, Pete, Peterus, Petey, Petr, Pierce, Pierre, Pierson, Pieter, Pietrek, Pietro, Piotr

Peyton (Old English) "from the warrior's estate."
Pate, Payton

Phil a short form of Filbert; Filmore; Philip.

Philip, Phillip (Greek) "lover of horses." Biblical: one of the Twelve Apostles.
Felipe, Filip, Filippo, Phil, Philipp, Phillipe, Phillipp, Pippo

Phineas (Hebrew) "oracle."
Pincas, Pinchas, Pincus

Pierce an English form of Peter. See also Percival.
Pearce, Peirce

Pierre a French form of Peter.

Plato (Greek) "broad-shouldered." Historical: a famous Greek philosopher.
Platon

Pollard (Old German) "cropped hair."
Pollerd

Pollock (Old English) a form of Pollux.
Polloch

Pollux (Greek) "crown."

Porter (Latin) "keeper of the gate."
Port, Portie, Porty

Powell (Celtic) "alert."

Prentice (Middle English) "apprentice."
Pren, Prent, Prentiss

Prescott (Old English) "from the priest's cottage."
Scott, Scottie, Scotty

Preston (Old English) "from the priest's estate."

Price (Welsh) "son of the ardent one."
Brice, Bryce, Pryce

Primo (Italian) "first; firstborn."

Prince (Latin) "chief, prince."
Prinz

Pryor (Latin) "head of a monastery; prior."
Prior, Pry

Purvis (English-French) "to provide food."

Putnam (Old English) "dweller by the pond."
Putnem

Quentin (Latin) "fifth; fifth child."
Quent, Quinn, Quint, Quintin, Quinton, Quintus

Quillan (Irish Gaelic) "cub."
Quill

Quincy (Old French) "from the fifth son's estate." See also Quentin.
Quinn

Quinlan (Irish Gaelic) "physically strong."
Quinn

Quinn (Irish Gaelic) "wise." A short form of Quentin; Quincy; Quinlan.

Rabi (Arabic) "breeze."
Rabbi

Radburn (Old English) "from the red stream."
Rad, Radborne, Radbourne, Raddie, Raddy

Radcliffe (Old English) "from the red cliff."
Rad, Raddie, Raddy

Radman (Slavic) "joy."
Radmen

Rafael a Spanish form of Raphael.
Rafe, Raffaello

Rafe a short form of Rafferty; Ralph; Raphael.

Rafferty (Irish Gaelic) "rich and prosperous."
Rafe, Raff, Raffarty

Rafi (Arabic) "exalting." Also a familiar form of Raphael.
Raffin

Raleigh (Old English) "from the deer meadow."
Lee, Leigh, Rawley

Ralph (Old English) "wolf-counselor."
Rafe, Raff, Ralf, Raoul, Rolf, Rolph

Ramón a Spanish form of Raymond.

Ramsay (Old English) "from the ram's island; from the raven's island."
Ram, Ramsey

Rance (African) "borrowed all."
Rancell, Ransell

Rand (Old English) "shield; warrior." A short form of Randall; Randolph.

Randall a modern form of Randolph.
Rand, Randal, Randell, Randy

Randolph (Old English) "shield-wolf."
Rand, Randal, Randall, Randell, Randolf, Randy

Randy a short form of Randall; Randolph.
Randi, Randie

Ranger (Old French) "guardian of the forest."
Rainger, Range

Ransom (Old English) "son of the shield."

Raoul a French form of Ralph; Rudolph.
Raul

Raphael (Hebrew) "God has healed." Biblical: an archangel.
Falito, Rafael, Rafaelle, Rafaello, Rafe, Ray

Ravi (Hindi) "sun."
Ravid, Raviv

Ray (Old French) "kingly; king's title." A short form of names beginning with the sound "ray."

Rayburn (Old English) "from the deer brook."
Burn, Burnie, Burny, Ray

Raymond (Old English) "mighty or wise protector."
Raimondo, Raimund, Raimundo, Ramón, Ray, Raymund, Reamonn

Raynor (Scandinavian) "mighty army."
Ragnar, Rainer, Ray, Rayner

Redford (Old English) "from the red river crossing."
Ford, Red, Redd

Redmond (Old German) "protecting counselor."
Redmund, Reddin

Reece (Welsh) "enthusiastic."
Rees, Reese, Rhys, Rice

Reed (Old English) "red-haired."
Read, Reade, Reid

Reeve (Middle English) "steward."

Regan (Irish Gaelic) "little king."
Reagan, Reagen, Regen

Reginald (Old English) "powerful and mighty."
Reg, Reggie, Reggis, Reginauld, Reinald, Reinaldo, Reinaldos, Reinhold, Reinold, Reinwald, Renault, René, Reynold, Reynolds, Rinaldo

Reid a form of Reed.

Remington (Old English) "from the raven estate."
Rem, Tony

Remus (Latin) "fast-moving." Mythological: Remus and his twin brother Romulus founded Rome.

René (French) "reborn." A French short form of Reginald (through Renault).

Reuben (Hebrew) "behold, a son."
Reuven, Rouvin, Rube, Ruben, Rubin, Ruby

Rex (Latin) "king."

Reynard (Old French) "fox"; (Old German) "mighty."
Ray, Raynard, Reinhard, Renard, Renaud, Rey

Reynold an English form of Reginald.
Renado, Renaldo, Renato, Reynolds

Rhett a Welsh form of Reece.

Rich a short form of Richard.
Richie, Richy, Ritchie

Richard (Old German) "powerful ruler."
Dick, Dickie, Dicky, Ric, Ricard, Ricardo, Riccardo, Rich, Richardo, Richart, Richie, Richy, Rick, Rickard, Rickert, Rickey, Ricki, Rickie, Ricky, Rico, Riki, Riocard, Ritchie

Richmond (Old German) "powerful protector." **Richmound**

Rick a short form of Richard; names containing the sound "rick." **Ric, Rickie, Ricky, Rik**

Rider (Old English) "horseman." **Rydder, Ryder**

Riley (Irish Gaelic) "valiant." **Reilly, Ryley**

Ring (Old English) "ring." **Ringo**

Riordan (Irish Gaelic) "bard, royal poet." **Dan, Dannie, Danny**

Rip (Dutch) "ripe, full-grown." A short form of Ripley. A familiar form of Robert (through Rupert).

Ripley (Old English) "from the shouter's meadow." **Lee, Leigh, Rip**

Roarke (Irish Gaelic) "famous ruler." **Rorke, Rourke**

Rob a short form of Robert. **Robb, Robbie, Robby**

Robert (Old English) "bright fame." **Bob, Bobbie, Bobby, Rab, Riobard, Rip, Rob, Robb, Robbie, Robby, Robers, Roberto, Robin, Rupert, Ruperto, Ruprecht**

Robin a familiar form of Robert. A short form of Robinson.

Robinson (English) "son of Robert." **Robin, Robinet**

Rochester (Old English) "from the stone camp." **Chester, Chet, Rock, Rockie, Rocky**

Rock (Old English) "from the rock." A short form of Rochester; Rockwell. **Rockie, Rocky**

Rockwell (Old English) "from the rocky spring."

Rocky a modern familiar form of Rochester; Rock; Rockwell. **Rockey**

Rod a short form of names beginning with "rod." **Rodd, Roddie, Roddy**

Roderick (Old German) "famous ruler." **Rod, Rodd, Roddie, Roddy, Roderic, Roderich, Roderigo, Rodrick, Rodrigo, Rodrique, Rory, Rurik, Ruy**

Rodger a form of Roger.

Rodman (Old English) "one who rides with a knight; famous man." **Rod, Rodd, Roddie, Roddy**

Rodney (Old English) "from the island clearing." **Rod, Rodd, Roddie, Roddy**

Roger (Old German) "famous spearman." **Rodge, Rodger, Rog, Rogerio, Rogers, Rüdiger, Ruggiero, Rutger, Ruttger**

Roland (Old German) "from the famous land." See also Orland. **Lannie, Lanny, Rolando, Roldan, Roley, Rolland, Rollie, Rollin, Rollins, Rollo, Rowland**

Rolf (Old German) "famous wolf." A German form of Ralph. A short form of Rudolph. **Rolfe, Rollo, Rolph**

Roman (Latin) "from Rome."
Roma, Romain

Romeo (Italian) "pilgrim to Rome." Literary: the hero of Shakespeare's *Romeo and Juliet*.

Romulus (Latin) "citizen of Rome." Mythological: Romulus and his twin brother Remus founded Rome.

Ron a short form of Aaron; Ronald.
Ronnie, Ronny

Ronald a Scottish form of Reginald.
Ron, Ronn, Ronnie, Ronny

Rooney (Irish Gaelic) "red-haired."
Rowan, Rowen, Rowney

Roosevelt (Old Dutch) "from the rose field." Historical: the name honors Franklin D. Roosevelt, thirty-second U.S. president, and Theodore Roosevelt, twenty-sixth U.S. president.

Rory (Irish Gaelic) "red king." An Irish familiar form of Roderick.

Roscoe (Scandinavian) "from the deer forest."
Rosco, Ross, Rossie, Rossy

Ross (Old French) "red"; (Scottish Gaelic) "headland." A short form of Roscoe.
Rosse, Rossie, Rossy

Roswald (Old English) "from a field of roses."
Ross, Roswell

Roth (Old German) "red hair."

Roy (Old French) "king." A short form of Royal; Royce.
Roi, Ruy

Royal (Old French) "royal."
Roy, Royall

Royce (Old English) "son of the king."
Roy

Rudd (Old English) "ruddy-complected." A short form of Rudyard.
Ruddie, Ruddy, Rudy

Rudolph (Old German) "famous wolf."
Raoul, Rodolfo, Rodolph, Rodolphe, Rolf, Rolfe, Rollo, Rolph, Rudie, Rudolf, Rudolfo, Rudy

Rudy a short form of names beginning with "rud."
Rudie

Rudyard (Old English) "from the red enclosure."
Rudd, Ruddie, Ruddy, Rudy

Ruford (Old English) "from the red ford."

Rufus (Latin) "red-haired."
Rufe

Rupert an Italian and Spanish form of Robert.

Ruskin (Old French) "red-haired."
Rush, Russ

Russ a short form of Cyrus; Ruskin; Russell.

Russell (French) "red-haired; fox-colored."
Russ, Rustie, Rusty

Rusty (French) "redhead." A short form of Russell.
Rustin

Rutherford (Old English) "from the cattle ford."
Ford

Rutledge (Old English) "from the red pool."
Rutter

Ryan (Irish Gaelic) "little king."
Ryon, Ryun

Salim (Arabic) "peace; safe."
Saleem, Salem

Salvatore (Italian) "savior."
Sal, Sallie, Sally, Salvador, Salvidor, Sauveur

Sam (Hebrew) "to hear." A short form of Samson; Samuel.
Sammie, Sammy, Shem

Samson (Hebrew) "like the sun." Biblical: the hero betrayed by Delilah.
Sam, Sammie, Sammy, Sampson, Sansón, Sansone, Shem

Samuel (Hebrew) "heard or asked of God." Biblical: a famous prophet and judge.
Sam, Sammie, Sammy, Samuele, Shem

Sanborn (Old English) "from the sandy brook."
Sandy

Sancho (Latin) "sanctified."
Sauncho

Sanders (Middle English) "son of Alexander."
Sander, Sanderson, Sandor, Sandy, Saunders, Saunderson

Sandy a familiar form of Alexander; a short form of names beginning with "san."

Sanford (Old English) "from the sandy river crossing."
Sandy

Sargent (Old French) "army officer."
Sarge, Sergeant, Sergent

Saul (Hebrew) "asked for." Biblical: the King of Israel and father of Jonathan; St. Paul is also called Saul of Tarsus.
Sol, Sollie, Solly, Zollie, Zolly

Sawyer (Middle English) "sawer of wood."
Saw, Sawyere

Saxon (Old English) "swordsman."
Sax, Saxe

Sayer (Welsh) "carpenter."
Say, Sayers, Sayre, Sayres

Schuyler (Dutch) "sheltering."
Sky, Skye, Skylar, Skyler

Scott (Old English) "Scotsman."
Scot, Scotti, Scottie, Scotty

Seamus an Irish form of James.
Seumas, Shamus

Sean an Irish form of John.
Shane, Shaughn, Shaun, Shawn

Sebastian (Latin) "venerated; majestic."
Bastian, Bastien, Sebastiano, Sébastien

Selby (Old English) "from the village by the mansion."

Seldon (Old English) "from the willow tree valley."
Don, Donnie, Donny, Selden, Shelden

Selig (Old German) "blessed."
Zelig

Selwyn (Old English) "friend from the palace."
Selwin, Winnie, Winny, Wyn, Wynn

Serge (Latin) "attendant."
Sergei, Sergio

Seth (Hebrew) "substitute; appointed." Biblical: the third son of Adam.

Seward (Old English) "victorious defender."
Siward

Sexton (Middle English) "church official; sexton."

Seymour (Old French) "from St. Maur." See also Maurice.
Morey, Morie, Morrie, Morry, See

Shalom (Hebrew) "peace."
Sholom, Solomon

Shamus an Irish form of James (through Seamus).

Shandy (Old English) "rambunctious."

Shane an Irish form of John (through Sean).
Shaine, Shayn, Shayne

Shannon (Irish Gaelic) "small and wise."
Shanan, Shannan

Shaw (Old English) "from the grove."

Shawn an Irish form of John (through Sean).

Shea (Irish Gaelic) "from the fairy fort."
Shae, Shay

Sheehan (Irish Gaelic) "little and peaceful."

Sheffield (Old English) "from the crooked field."
Field, Fields, Sheff, Sheffie, Sheffy

Shelby (Old English) "from the ledge estate."
Shell, Shelley, Shelly

Sheldon (Old English) "from the farm on the ledge."
Shell, Shelley, Shelly, Shelton

Shelley a familiar form of Shelby; Sheldon. Literary: the name honors the poet Percy Bysshe Shelley.
Shell, Shelly

Shepherd (Old English) "shepherd."
Shep, Shepard, Sheppard, Shepperd

Sherborn (Old English) "from the clear brook."
Sherborne, Sherburn, Sherburne

Sheridan (Irish Gaelic) "wild man."
Dan, Dannie, Danny

Sherlock (Old English) "fair-haired."
Sherlocke, Shurlock, Shurlocke

Sherman (Old English) "shearer."
Man, Mannie, Manny, Sherm, Shermie, Shermy

Sherwin (Middle English) "swift runner."
Sherwynd, Win, Winn, Winnie, Winny, Wyn

Sherwood (Old English) "from the bright forest."
Shurwood, Wood, Woodie, Woody

Sid a short form of Sidney.

Sidney (Old French) "from St. Denis."
Sid, Sidnee, Syd, Sydney

Siegfried (Old German) "victorious peace."
Siffre, Sig, Sigfrid, Sigfried, Sigvard

Sigmund (Old German) "victorious protector."
Sig, Sigismondo, Sigismund, Sigismundo, Sigsmond

Silas (Latin) "Silvanus (the forest god)."
Silvain, Silvan, Silvano, Silvanus, Silvio, Sylas, Sylvan

Silvester a form of Sylvester.

Simon (Hebrew) "he who hears." Biblical: one of the Twelve Disciples.
Si, Sim, Simeon, Simmonds, Simone, Syman, Symon

Sinclair (Old French) "from St. Clair."
Clair, Clare, Sinclare

Skelly (Irish Gaelic) "storyteller."
Skell

Skip (Scandinavian) "shipmaster."
Skipp, Skipper, Skippie, Skippy, Skipton

Slade (Old English) "child of the valley."

Sloan (Irish Gaelic) "warrior."
Sloane

Smith (Old English) "blacksmith."
Smitty

Solomon (Hebrew) "peaceful." Biblical: a King of Israel, famous for his wisdom.
Salmon, Salomo, Salomon, Salomone, Sol, Sollie, Solly, Zollie, Zolly

Somerset (Old English) "from the place of the summer settlers."

Spark (Middle English) "happy."
Sparke, Sparkie, Sparky

Spencer (Middle English) "dispenser of provisions."
Spence, Spense, Spenser

Sprague (Old French) "lively."

Stacy (Medieval) "stable; prosperous."
Stace, Stacee, Stacey

Stafford (Old English) "from the riverbank landing place."
Staffard, Staford

Stan a short form of names containing "stan."

Stanford (Old English) "from the rocky ford."
Ford, Stan, Standford, Stanfield

Stanislaus (Slavic) "stand of glory."
Stan, Stanislas, Stanislaw

Stanley (Old English) "from the rocky meadow."
Stan, Stanleigh, Stanly

Stanton (Old English) "from the stony farm."
Stan, Stanwood

Stephen (Greek) "crown."
Esteban, Estevan, Étienne, Stefan, Stefano, Steffen, Stephan, Stephanus, Steve, Steven, Stevie, Stevy

Sterling (Old English) "valuable."
Stirling

Sterne (Middle English) "austere."
Stearn, Stearne, Stern

Steve a short form of Stephen.
Stevie, Stevy

Steven a form of Stephen.

Stewart a form of Stuart.
Steward

Stillman (Old English) "quiet man."
Stillmann

Strephon (Greek) "one who turns."
Strep, Strephonn, Strepphon

Stuart (Old English) "caretaker; steward." Historical: the name of many British kings.
Steward, Stewart, Stu

Styles (Old English) "from the stiles."

Sullivan (Irish Gaelic) "black-eyed."
Sully

Sumner (Middle English) "church officer; summoner."

Sutherland (Scandinavian) "from the southern land."
Sutherlan

Sutton (Old English) "from the southern town."

Sven (Scandinavian) "youth."
Svend, Swen

Sylvester (Latin) "from the woods."
Silvester, Sly

Tab (Middle English) "drummer."
Tabb, Tabbie, Tabby, Taber, Tabor

Tabib (Turkish) "physician."

Tad a Polish familiar form of Thaddeus (through Taddeusz).

Tadeo (Spanish, Latin) "praise."
Tadeas, Tades

Talbot (Old German-French) "valley-bright."
Talbert, Tallie, Tally

Tanner (Old English) "leather worker, tanner."
Tan, Tann, Tanney, Tannie, Tanny

Taro (Japanese) "first-born male."

Tate (Middle English) "cheerful."
Tait, Taite

Tavish (Irish Gaelic) "twin."
Tav, Tavis, Tevis

Tayib (Indian) "good or delicate."

Taylor (Middle English) "tailor."
Tailor

Teague (Irish Gaelic) "bard."
Teagan, Teak

Ted a familiar form of names beginning with "ed"; "ted."
Tedd, Teddie, Teddy, Tedman, Tedmund

Templeton (Old English) "from the town of the temple."
Temp, Temple

Terence (Latin) "smooth." Literary: the name honors the great Latin poet.
Tarrance, Terencio, Terrance, Terrence, Terry

Terrill (Old German) "belonging to Thor; martial."
Terrel, Terrell, Tirrell

Terry a familiar form of Terence.
Terri

Thaddeus (Greek) "courageous"; (Latin) "praiser." Biblical: one of the Twelve Apostles.
Tad, Tadd, Taddeo, Taddeusz, Tadeo, Tadio, Thad, Thaddäus

Thane (Old English) "attendant warrior; thane."
Thain, Thaine, Thayne

Thatcher (Old English) "roof thatcher."
Thacher, Thatch, Thaxter

Thayer (Old French) "from the nation's army."
Thay

Theo a short form of names beginning with "theo."

Theobald (Old German) "people's prince."
Ted, Tedd, Teddie, Teddy, Thébault, Theo, Thibaud, Thibaut, Tibold, Tiebold, Tiebout, Toiboid, Tybalt

Theodore (Greek) "gift of God."
Feodor, Teador, Ted, Tedd, Teddie, Teddy, Teodoor, Teodor, Teodoro, Theo, Theodor, Théodore, Tudor

Theodoric (Old German) "powerful people; ruler of the people." The name is not related to Theodore.
Derek, Dieter, Dietrich, Dirk, Ted, Tedd, Teddie, Teddy, Teodorico, Thedric, Thedrick, Theo

Thomas (Aramaic-Hebrew) "twin." Biblical: one of the Twelve Apostles.
Tam, Tamas, Tammie, Tammy, Thom, Thoma, Tom, Tomás, Tomaso, Tome, Tomkin, Tomlin, Tommie, Tommy

Thor (Scandinavian) "thunder." Mythological: the thunder god.
Thorin, Thorvald, Tore, Torin, Torre, Tyrus

Thorndike (Old English) "from the thorny embankment."
Thorn, Thornie, Thorny

Thornton (Old English) "from the thorny farm."
Thorn, Thornie, Thorny

Thorpe (Old English) "from the village."

Thurston (Scandinavian) "Thor's stone."
Thorstein, Thorsten, Thurstan

Tim a short form of Timothy.
Timmie, Timmy

Timothy (Greek) "honoring God."
Tim, Timmie, Timmy, Timofei, Timoteo, Timothée, Timotheus, Tymon, Tymothy

Titus (Greek) "of the giants."
Tito, Titos

Tobias (Hebrew) "the Lord is good."
Tobe, Tobiah, Tobie, Tobin, Tobit, Toby

Toby a familiar form of Tobias.
Tobie

Todd (Middle English) "fox."
Toddie, Toddy

Tom a short form of Thomas
Tommie, Tommy

Tony a familiar form of Anthony; names ending in "ton."
Toni, Tonnie

Torin (Irish Gaelic) "chief."
Thorfinn, Thorstein

Torrance (Irish Gaelic) "from the knolls."
Tore, Torey, Torin, Torr, Torrence, Torrey, Torrin, Torry

Townsend (Old English) "from the town's end."
Town, Towney, Townie, Towny

Tracy (Irish Gaelic) "battler"; (Latin) "courageous."
Trace, Tracey, Tracie

Trahern (Welsh) "strong as iron."
Tray

Travis (Old French) "at the crossroads."
Traver, Travers, Travus

Tremain (Celtic) "from the house of stone."
Tremaine, Tremayne

Trent (Latin) "torrent."
Trenton

Trevor (Irish Gaelic) "prudent."
Trefor, Trev, Trevar, Trever

Trey (Middle English) "three, the third."

Trip, Tripp (Middle English, French) "to dance or hop."

Tristan (Welsh) "sorrowful." Literary: a famous knight in the Arthurian legends.
Tris, Tristam, Tristram

Troy (Irish Gaelic) "foot soldier."

Truman (Old English) "faithful man." Historical: the name honors Harry S Truman, thirty-third U.S. president.
Trueman, Trumaine, Trumann

Tucker (Old English) "fuller or tucker of cloth."
Tuck, Tuckie, Tucky

Tully (Irish Gaelic) "he who lives with the peace of God."
Tull, Tulley

Turner (Latin) "one who works the lathe."

Tut (Arabic) "strong and courageous." Historical: the name honors Tutankhamen, the Egyptian king.
Tutt

Ty a short form of names beginning with "ty."

Tyler (Old English) "maker of tiles."
Tiler, Ty, Tye

Tynan (Irish Gaelic) "dark."
Ty, Tye

Tyrone (Greek) "sovereign"; (Irish Gaelic) "land of Owen."
Ty, Tye

Tyrus an English form of Thor.
Ty, Tye

Tyson (Old French) "firebrand."
Ty, Tye

Udell (Old English) "from the yew tree valley."
Del, Dell, Udale, Udall

Ulric (Old German) "wolf-ruler."
Alaric, Ric, Rick, Rickie, Ricky, Ulrich, Ulrick

Ulysses (Latin-Greek) "Odysseus; wrathful." Literary: the hero of Homer's *Odyssey*.
Ulick, Ulises

Upton (Old English) "from the upper town."

Urban (Latin) "from the city; courteous."
Urbain, Urbano, Urbanus

Uriah (Hebrew) "Jehovah is my light." Biblical: the husband of Bathsheba and a captain in David's army.
Uri, Yuri, Yuria

Uriel (Hebrew) "God is my flame."
Uri, Yuri

Uziel (Hebrew) "strength; a mighty force."

Vail (Old English) "from the valley."
Bail, Bale, Vale, Valle

Valentine (Latin) "strong; healthy."
Val, Valentijn, Valentin, Valentino

Van (Dutch) "of noble descent." A short form of many Dutch surnames.

Vance (Middle English) "thresher."

Vasilis (Greek) "knightly, magnificent."
Vasileior, Vasos

Vassily (Slavic, German) "unwavering protector."
Vas, Vasilek, Vasya, Vasyuta

Vaughn (Welsh) "small."
Vaughan, Von

Vern a short form of Vernon.

Vernon (Latin) "springlike; youthful."
Lavern, Vern, Verne, Verney

Victor (Latin) "conqueror."
Vic, Vick, Victoir, Vittorio

Vincent (Latin) "conquering."
Vin, Vince, Vincents, Vincenty, Vincenz, Vinnie, Vinny

Vinny a familiar form of Vincent.
Vin, Vinnie

Vinson (Old English) "the conqueror's son."
Vin, Vinnie, Vinny

Virgil (Latin) "rod or staff bearer."
Verge, Vergil, Virge, Virgle, Virgilio

Vito (Latin) "alive."
Vite

Vladimir (Slavic) "powerful prince."
Vladamir

Wade (Old English) "advancer; from the river crossing."
Wadsworth

Wainwright (Old English) "wagonmaker."
Wain, Wayne, Wright

Waite (Middle English) "guard."

Wakefield (Old English) "from the wet field."
Field, Wake

Waldemar (Old German) "powerful and famous."
Valdemar, Wald, Waldo, Wallie, Wally

Walden (Old English) "from the woods."
Waldon

Waldo (Old German) "ruler." A familiar form of Oswald; Waldemar.
Wald, Wallie, Wally

Waldron (Old English) "ruler."
Waldo

Walker (Old English) "thickener of cloth, fuller."
Wallie, Wally

Wallace (Old English) "Welshman."
Wallache, Wallas, Wallie, Wallis, Wally, Walsh, Welch, Welsh

Wally a familiar form of names beginning with "wal."
Wallie

Walt a short form of Walter; Walton.

Walter (Old German) "powerful warrior."
Gauthier, Gualterio, Gualtiero, Wallie, Wally, Walt, Walther, Wat

Walton (Old English) "from the walled town."
Wallie, Wally, Walt

Ward (Old English) "guardian."
Warde, Warden, Worden

Warner (Old German) "armed defender."
Werner, Wernher

Warren (Old German) "defender."
Ware, Waring

Washington (Old English) "from the town of one known for astuteness." Historical: the name honors George Washington, first U.S. president.
Wash

Waverly (Old English) "from the meadow of quaking aspen trees."
Lee, Leigh, Waverley

Wayland (Old English) "from the land by the road."
Land, Way, Waylan, Waylen, Waylin, Waylon, Weylin

Wayne (Old English) "wagoner." A short form of Wainwright.

Webb (Old English) "weaver."
Weber, Webster

Welby (Old German) "from the farm by the spring."
Welbie

Wells (Old English) "from the springs."

Wendell (Old German) "wanderer."
Wendall, Wendel

Werner a German form of Warner.
Wernher

Wes a short form of names beginning with "wes."

Wesley (Old English) "from the western meadow."
Lee, Leigh, Wes, Westleigh, Westley

Westbrook (Old English) "from the western brook." **Brook, Brooke, Wes, West, Westbrooke**

Weston (Old English) "from the western estate." **Wes, West**

Wheeler (Old English) "wheelmaker."

Whitman (Old English) "white-haired man." **Whit**

Whitney (Old English) "from the white island; from fair water." **Whit**

Whittaker (Old English) "from the white field." **Whit, Whitaker**

Whitby (Scandinavian) "from the white dwellings."

Wilbur a German form of Gilbert. **Wilbert, Wilburt**

Wildon (Old English) "from the wooded hill." **Wilden, Willdon**

Wiley (Old English) "from the water meadow; from Will's meadow." **Willey, Wylie**

Wilfred (Old German) "resolute and peaceful." **Wilfrid, Will, Willie, Willy**

Will a short form of names beginning with the sound "will." **Willie, Willy**

Willard (Old German) "resolutely brave." **Will, Willie, Willy**

William (Old German) "determined guardian." **Bill, Billie, Billy, Guglielmo, Guillaume, Guillermo, Liam, Wilek, Wilhelm, Will, Willem, Willi, Willie, Willis, Willy, Wilmar, Wilmer**

Wilton (Old English) "from the farm by the spring." **Will, Willie, Willy, Wilt**

Win a short form of names containing "win"; "wyn." **Winn, Winnie, Winny**

Winfield (Old English) "from the friendly field." **Field, Win, Winifield, Winn, Winnie, Winny, Wyn**

Winslow (Old English) "from the friend's hill." **Win, Winn, Winnie, Winny, Wyn**

Winston (Old English) "from the friendly town." **Win, Winn, Winnie, Winny, Winstonn, Wyn**

Winthrop (Old English) "from the wine village." **Win, Winn, Winnie, Winny, Wyn**

Witha (Arabic) "handsome."

Wolfgang (Old German) "advancing wolf." Historical: the name honors composer Wolfgang Amadeus Mozart. **Wolf, Wolfie, Wolfy**

Woodrow (Old English) "from the passage in the woods." **Wood, Woodie, Woodman, Woody**

Woody a familiar form of names containing "wood." **Wood, Woodie**

Worth (Old English) "from the farmstead." A short form of names ending in "worth." **Worthington, Worthy**

Wright (Old English) "carpenter." A short form of Wainwright.

Wyatt (Old French) "little warrior." **Wiatt, Wye**

Wylie (Old English) "charming."
Lee, Leigh, Wiley, Wye

Wyndham (Scottish Gaelic) "from the village near the winding road."
Windham

Wynn (Welsh) "fair."
Winn, Winnie, Winny

Xanthus (Latin) "golden-haired."

Xavier (Arabic) "bright."
Javier, Xever

Xenophon (Greek) "strange voice."
Xeno, Zennie

Xenos (Greek) "stranger."

Xerxes (Persian) "ruler." Historical: the name of many Persian emperors.
Zerk

Ximenes a Spanish form of Simon.
Xymenes, Ximenez

Xylon (Greek) "from the forest."

Yale (Old English) "from the corner of the land."

Yancy (North American Indian) "Englishman."
Yance, Yancey, Yank, Yankee

Yardley (Old English) "from the enclosed meadow."
Lee, Leigh, Yard

Yehudi (Hebrew) "praise of the Lord."
Yehudit

York (Old English) "estate of the boar."
Yorke, Yorker

Yule (Old English) "December, January; born at Yuletide."
Euell, Ewell, Yul

Yuma (North American Indian) "son of a chief."

Yuri a familiar form of Uriah.

Yves a French form of Ivar. The name may also mean "knight of the lion."
Ives

Zachariah (Hebrew) "the Lord's remembrance."
Zach, Zacharia, Zacharias, Zack, Zackariah, Zak, Zechariah

Zachary (Hebrew) "Jehovah hath remembered."
Zacarias, Zaccaria, Zach, Zachariah, Zacharias, Zacharie, Zacherie, Zachery, Zack, Zak, Zakarias, Zechariah, Zeke

Zane an English form of John.

Zared (Hebrew) "ambush."

Zebadiah (Hebrew) "the Lord's gift."
Zeb, Zebedee

Zebulon (Hebrew) "dwelling place."
Zeb, Zebulen

Zedekiah (Hebrew) "God is mighty and just."
Zed

Zeke a short form of Ezekiel; Zachary.

Zephaniah (Hebrew) "treasured by the Lord."
Zeph, Zephan

Zollie, Zolly familiar forms of Saul; Solomon.

Best Baby Name Worksheet

Mom's Favorite Names				Dad's Favorite Names			
rating	girls	rating	boys	rating	girls	rating	boys

Final Choice Worksheet

Girls' Names

rating	first	middle	last
___	___	___	___
___	___	___	___
___	___	___	___
___	___	___	___
___	___	___	___
___	___	___	___
___	___	___	___

Boys' Names

rating	first	middle	last
___	___	___	___
___	___	___	___
___	___	___	___
___	___	___	___
___	___	___	___
___	___	___	___

The 15 things to consider: namesakes, nationality, religion, gender, number of names, sounds, rhythms, pronunciation, spelling, popularity, uniqueness, stereotypes, initials, nicknames, meanings

Pregnancy, Childbirth, and the Newborn
by Simkin, Whalley, and Keppler
If you only buy one childbirth guide, this should be the one. It's the most complete–it tells and shows (with over 100 photos, illustrations, and charts) how to prepare yourself for a healthy, positive birth experience. It covers nutrition, exercise, labor comfort measures, anesthesia choices, birth, breastfeeding, and new baby care. Created by the Childbirth Education Association of Seattle, childbirth experts call it their "bible."
Order #1169

The Birth Partner's Handbook
by Carl Jones
Labor room companions can use this book as a childbirth class refresher course during the ninth month, and as a bedside manual that clearly spells out "what to do when." Jones, a leading childbirth educator, covers every potentially troublesome situation that may arise. A must-have book, if only for the emergency delivery instructions.
Order #1309

Getting Organized for Your New Baby
by Maureen Bard
Here's the fastest way to get organized for pregnancy, childbirth, and new baby care. Busy expectant parents love the checklists, forms, schedules, charts, and hints in this book because they make getting ready so much easier.
Order #1229

First-Year Baby Care
edited by Paula Kelly, M.D.
Since babies don't come with an "owner's manual" we created one to help you anticipate and handle your new baby's basic needs without worry. This helpful handbook covers feeding, bathing, first aid, health childproofing, and sleeping (good luck!). Newly revised, this book gives new parents the techniques and confidence they need.
Order #1119

Hi Mom! Hi Dad!
by Lynn Johnston

Most new parents don't think the first 12 months of parenthood is a laughing matter ... till they read this collection of 101 cartoons by Lynn Johnston. There's something about sleepness nights and babbling days that seems a lot funnier in a cartoon book.

Order #1139

Grandma Knows Best, But No One Ever Listens
by Mary McBride

Mary McBride offers much-needed advice for **new** grandmas on how to

- Show baby photos to anyone at any time
- Get out of babysitting ... or if stuck, to housebreak the kids before they wreck the house
- Advise the daughter-in-law without being **without** being banned from her home.

The perfect give for grandma, it's "harder to **put** down than a new grandchild." Phyllis Diller

Order #4009

Moms Say the Funniest Things!
by Bruce Lansky

Bruce Lansky has collected all the greatest lines moms have ever used to deal with "emergencies" like getting the kids out of bed in the morning, cleaned, dressed, to school, to the dinner table, undressed, and back to bed. It includes all-time winners such as: "Put on clean underwear–you never know when you'll be in an accident," and, "If God had wanted you to fool around He would have written 'The Ten Suggestions.'" A fun gift for mom and the rest of the family, too.

Order #4280

Dads Say the Dumbest Things!
by Bruce Lansky and Ken Jones

Lansky and Jones have collected all the greatest lines dads have ever used to get kids to stop fighting in the car, feed the pet, turn off the TV while doing homework, and get home before curfew. It includes winners such as: "What do you want a pet for–you've got a sister," and, "When I said 'feed the goldfish,' I didn't mean feed them to the cat." A fun gift for dad and the rest of the family, too.

Order #4220

Feed Me! I'm Yours
by Vicki Lansky
This classic cookbook for mothers of infants, toddlers, and tots contains over 200 time-tested recipes for making baby food from scratch and preparing nutritional snacks for preschoolers. Spiral bound to lay flat–a handy feature since many mothers say they "live out of it." No wonder it has sold over 2.5 million copies.
Order #1109

Practical Parenting Tips
by Vicky Lansky
Here's the #1-selling collection of helpful hints for parents of babies and small children. It contains 1001 parent-tested tips for dealing with diaper rash, nighttime crying, toilet training, temper tantrums, and traveling with tots that will help you save trouble, time, and money.
Order #1179

The Best Baby Shower Book
by Courtney Cooke
Who says baby showers have to be dull? This contemporary guide is packed with planning tips, decorating ideas, recipes, and activities that are fun without being juvenile.
Order #1239

The Working Woman's Guide to Breastfeeding
by Nancy Dana and Anne Price
This indispensable guide for working breastfeeding mothers tells you how to balance breastfeeding and your job. It's the best single source of practical information about pumping and storing breast milk.
Order #1259

Order Form

Quantity	Title	Author	Order No.	Unit Cost	Total
	Baby & Child Medical Care	Hart, T.	1159	$8.00	
	Baby Name Personality Survey, The	Lansky/Sinrod	1270	$7.00	
	Best Baby Name Book, The	Lansky, B.	1029	$5.00	
	Best Baby Shower, The	Cooke, C.	1239	$6.00	
	Birth Partner's Handbook	Jones, C.	1309	$6.00	
	Dads Say the Dumbest Things!	Lansky, B	4220	$6.00	
	David, We're Pregnant!	Johnston, L.	1049	$6.00	
	Discipline w/out Shouting, Spanking	Wyckoff/Unell	1079	$6.00	
	Do They Ever Grow Up?	Johnston, L.	1089	$6.00	
	Feed Me! I'm Yours	Lansky, V.	1109	$8.00	
	First-Year Baby Care	Kelly, P.	1119	$7.00	
	Getting Organized for Your New Baby	Bard, M.	1229	$5.00	
	Grandma Knows Best	McBride, M.	4009	$5.00	
	Hi, Mom! Hi, Dad!	Johnston, L.	1139	$6.00	
	Moms Say the Funniest Things!	Lansky, B.	4280	$6.00	
	Pregnancy, Childbirth, and the Newborn	Simkin/Whalley/Keppler	1169	$12.00	
	Practical Parenting Tips	Lansky, V.	1179	$7.00	
	Visualizations for an Easier Childbirth	Jones, C.	1330	$6.00	
	Working Woman's Guide to Breastfeeding	Dana/Price	1259	$7.00	
				Subtotal	
				Shipping and Handling (see below)	
				MN residents add 6.5% sales tax	
				Total	

YES, please send me the books indicated above. Add $1.50 shipping and handling for the first book and $.50 for each additional book. Add $2.00 to total for books shipped to Canada. Overseas postage will be billed. Allow up to 4 weeks for delivery. Send check or money order payable to Meadowbrook Press. No cash or C.O.D.'s please. Prices subject to change without notice. **Quantity discounts available upon request.**

Send book(s) to:

Name _____ Phone _____

Address _____

City _____ State _____ Zip _____

Payment via:

☐ Check or money order payable to Meadowbrook Press. (No cash or C.O.D.'s please) Amt. enclosed $ _____

☐ Visa (for orders over $10.00 only.)   ☐ MasterCard (for orders over $10.00 only).

Account # _____ Signature _____ Exp. Date ____

You can also phone us for orders of $10.00 or more at 1-800-338-2232.

A **FREE** Meadowbrook Press catalog is available upon request.

Mail to: Meadowbrook Inc., 18318 Minnetonka Blvd., Deephaven, MN 55391

(612) 473-5400   Toll-Free 1-800-338-2232   FAX (612) 475-0736